I0521114

OUT OF THE LOOP, INTO THE ALGORITHM

How I Finally Made Friends with AI

By

WANJIKU KAMAU

DEDICATION

For Elle, who gave me hope to reimagine my future. For Champ, who kept me grounded when everything felt uncertain. For my mother, who taught me that my voice matters. And for all the family and friends who believed in me during the pivot—you know who you are.

FOREWORD

There comes a moment in every life when the ground beneath you shifts. The career you thought defined you, the identity you leaned on for stability, the rhythm of your days: they all suddenly feel uncertain. And in that moment, fear and opportunity collide. You can choose to shrink into the discomfort, or you can lean forward, curious and unafraid, and discover a new version of yourself waiting on the other side.

I have watched Wanjiku Kamau inhabit exactly that space. I have watched her move through it with courage, clarity, and relentless optimism. I have seen her take a career built at some of the most powerful tech companies in the world and, when life handed her a detour in the form of an unexpected layoff, turn it into a launchpad for reinvention. Watching her do this has been nothing short of inspiring.

Wanjiku's story is not about mastery or perfection. It is about curiosity, experimentation, and the audacity to say: I may be out of the loop now, but I refuse to stay there. From the Sacramento airport gate, Googling acronyms and feeling behind, to building two businesses, starting a podcast, and becoming a trusted AI guide for friends and colleagues, she has turned a moment of uncertainty into a masterclass in transformation.

This book, Out of the Loop, Into the Algorithm, is for anyone who has ever nodded along while everyone else seemed to get it: those moments when work, life, or technology feels like it's moving faster than you can keep up. It is a guide for women in transition, for professionals navigating disruption, and for anyone who has questioned whether they can catch up, adapt, or reinvent themselves.

What makes Wanjiku's journey so compelling, and why this book resonates, is her honesty about the messy middle. She shares the failures as openly as the wins: the "spectacular failures" with AI projects that didn't go as planned, the moments of exhaustion, the self-doubt, and the very real fear of stepping into uncharted territory. And then she shows us how to move forward anyway. She shows us how to turn tools, curiosity, and persistence into transformation.

As you read, you will discover frameworks that are as practical as they are empowering. You will learn how to collaborate with AI without losing your voice, how to set boundaries that protect your humanity, and how to take action even when confidence wavers. But more importantly, you will see how Wanjiku lives these principles in real time, proving that reinvention is possible, accessible, and deeply human.

Her story has inspired me personally in ways I didn't expect. Seeing Wanjiku navigate the complexity of career, technology, and identity and emerge thriving rather than just surviving gave me courage in my own moments of uncertainty. She has a rare gift: the ability to lift others even as she charts her own path. This book carries that gift to every reader who opens it.

Lean in. Let her story remind you that being "out of the loop" is not a failure. It is an invitation. An invitation to curiosity, to growth, to courage. To a life where setbacks become pivots, fear becomes fuel, and you become the author of your next chapter.

Because if Wanjiku can sit at that gate, unsure and overwhelmed, and walk into the unknown and come out the other side more powerful, more resilient, more herself, then so can you.

—**Tamara Srzentić**
First Digital Minister of Montenegro
Digital and Open Data Reform Lead, California State Government

A NOTE FROM WANJIKU

This book tells my real story: the messy, uncertain, sometimes hilarious journey of figuring out AI. The conversations and events actually happened, though I've changed some names and details to protect people's privacy. Everyone else who appears by name gave me permission to share their part of the story.

Throughout the book, I mention various AI tools, platforms, and companies. I'm sharing what worked (and didn't work) for me, not telling you what to buy. I don't have any financial relationships with these companies. I'm just a person who used their products and learned along the way. Your mileage may vary, and that's completely okay.

This book isn't professional advice: legal, financial, medical, or otherwise. It's one person's experience learning something new. If you need expert guidance, please consult actual experts in those fields.

Contents

DEDICATION iii

FOREWORD iv

A NOTE FROM WANJIKU vii

INTRODUCTION 1

CHAPTER 1: AT THE GATE 4

CHAPTER 2: EVERYONE GOT THE MEMO BUT ME 8

CHAPTER 3: HI, CHATGPT 17

CHAPTER 4: SPECTACULAR FAILURES 25

CHAPTER 5: FINDING MY TEACHERS 31

CHAPTER 6: FROM SEARCH TO FRIENDSHIP 42

CHAPTER 7: MY FIRST REAL WIN 49

CHAPTER 8: THE NETWORKING NINJA'S PROBLEM 57

CHAPTER 9: LOSING THE PLAYBOOK 64

CHAPTER 10: FIVE FRIENDS, FIVE TOOLS 70

CHAPTER 11: CONTEXT IS EVERYTHING 79

CHAPTER 12: THE TIMES SQUARE TEST 87

CHAPTER 13: BUILDING SOMETHING THAT LASTS 94

CHAPTER 14: WHEN AI FAILS LOUDLY 106

CHAPTER 15: WAIT, YOU'RE ASKING ME? 116

CHAPTER 16: YOUR TURN 124

EPILOGUE 132

ACKNOWLEDGEMENTS 134

RESOURCES & QUICK REFERENCE 138

ABOUT THE AUTHOR 141

CONNECT WITH WANJIKU 143

DISCLAIMERS 145

INTRODUCTION

You know that feeling when everyone's talking about something and you're just nodding along, pretending you get it? That was me with AI for the longest time.

It seemed like overnight, everyone had an opinion. Your cousin was posting on Facebook about robots taking over. Your neighbor casually mentioned ChatGPT like it was nothing. Even your grandmother asked if she should be worried about "that artificial intelligence thing" she saw on the news.

And there you are, wondering: What exactly is AI? Should I care? Am I missing something important?

If you've ever felt lost, late, or left out of the AI conversation, hello. This book is for you.

And honestly, I was right there with you, smiling and nodding, hoping no one noticed I had no idea what we were talking about. Months ago, I couldn't have explained AI to save my life. I was the one frantically Googling acronyms mid-conversation, just trying to keep up, feeling like everyone else had gotten some memo I'd missed.

Maybe you're starting from a different place than I was. Maybe you're employed but curious, or tech-savvy but AI-confused. Wherever you are, the feeling of being behind is probably the same.

But here's what I learned: you don't need to be a computer genius to understand this stuff. What I didn't realize back then was how quickly things would change once I stopped pretending and started experimenting. Curiosity, it turns out, is the only credential that matters.

What Actually Happens in This Book

This isn't a textbook. It's the story of how I went from being completely confused to finally making sense of AI for myself. Not because I'm special, but because I stopped trying to learn it the "right" way and started figuring out what actually worked for me.

You'll see all the times I messed up—like when I kept asking ChatGPT to remember things from our previous conversations, getting frustrated that its memory was so limited. You'll experience that moment when things finally clicked for me. And I'll share simple ways to think about AI that don't involve confusing jargon. I'll show you how I started using it for real things in my everyday life, and why it's not nearly as scary as the internet makes it seem.

By the end, you might find yourself a little less intimidated by the whole topic. Maybe you'll try asking ChatGPT a question without feeling awkward about it. Maybe you'll understand enough to hold your own in a conversation when someone brings it up. You might even catch yourself explaining to a friend that it's really not that complicated.

What This Isn't

This isn't a book that will teach you how to build apps or become a programmer. I'm not here to convince you that AI will completely change your entire life (though it might help with some of the annoying stuff). And I'm definitely not going to pretend I have all the answers.

This is simply one person's journey from confusion to clarity.

My Story Starts with Feeling Lost

Here's how it actually happened for me.

I was sitting in the Sacramento airport with my dog, Champ, feeling like my whole career had just fallen apart. I'd lost my job, and for the first time in years, I had no idea what came next.

That's when I finally stopped avoiding all the AI talk and decided to figure out what the fuss was about. Not because I had some big plan, but because I suddenly had time and I was curious.

What happened next surprised me. And if it could happen for someone as lost as I was, it can probably happen for you, too.

So, let's start at the beginning.

CHAPTER 1

AT THE GATE

At the Sacramento airport gate, with the low hum of conversations and rolling luggage around us, it was just me and my dog, Champ, waiting for our flight home to New York. I'd just said goodbye to my family—including a kiss for my newborn niece, Elle—and now Champ curled up beside me, his head resting on my thigh, his tongue poking out the way it always does. Calm, steady, content. Airports didn't faze him; he could ride escalators and elevators like a pro. Butterflies, on the other hand, terrified him. Sitting there with him, it almost felt like he carried the calm I couldn't quite find for myself.

On paper, my career looked solid. Siemens. Intel. Google. An MBA. These companies had brought stability to an industry that rarely offers it. In just under four years at Google, I'd found myself in a world I couldn't have imagined—working with AI tools like Gemini and NotebookLM that most people had never heard of, but somehow never really exploring what they could do for me personally.

My days were spent preparing endless presentations about data center strategy across regions from Latin America to Europe, making the case for resource allocation and trying to anticipate what different markets would need. It was complex, important work that I genuinely found rewarding, even when I wasn't always in the room where the final decisions got made. But the pace had taken more than I wanted to admit. The hours, the constant pressure, the way the role seemed to expand in every direction. I'd started wondering if I needed to take a mental health break, if I could keep going like this much longer.

Earlier that year, everything changed in a day.

I knew something was off that whole week. The energy had shifted in a way I couldn't quite name. That Wednesday morning, I messaged a colleague: "Are layoffs happening today?" They messaged back: "I think so."

Then I got the call.

I knew before the conversation even started. The layoff was presented as an opportunity to find another internal role or take a severance package. I pretended to feel sad, asked the right questions, and nodded at the right moments. But inside? I wanted to dance.

The first person I called was my mom. "I'm so relieved," I told her, and I meant it. That night, I slept ten hours straight—like I hadn't truly slept in years.

The idea of walking away gutted me. But the truth? It also brought a quiet sense of relief that I couldn't ignore.

Relief doesn't erase the stakes, though. My career had always been my anchor, my stability, my identity. I hadn't realized how much I'd miss being able to say "*I work at Google.*" It was code for success, a badge that meant something to my family, to people I'd just met. "*This is my friend Wanjiku. She works at Google.*" It carried weight I hadn't even realized I was carrying. And here I was, sitting at a gate, realizing that the

5

anchor was slipping. For the first time in my career, I didn't know what came next.

Before I left Sacramento, I'd watched Elle sleeping in my brother's arms—barely a month old—and thought about legacy. Her tiny fingers curled into fists, that newborn frown that made her look like she was solving complex equations in her dreams. My brother looked exhausted but mesmerized, and Sandra, still glowing in those early weeks of motherhood, looked at Elle like she couldn't believe this tiny person was real. "She's going to know you," my brother said quietly. "Not just as the aunt who flies in once a year from New York. Really know you."

That hit differently than I expected.

What kind of aunt did I want to be? The one she saw once a year when I flew in from whatever company was consuming my life? Or someone who built something that gave me the flexibility to be present for the moments that mattered?

Elle's tiny sleeping face stayed with me as I sat there at the gate, catching up on emails and messages. Friends sending job leads, recruiters pinging me on LinkedIn, networking invites stacking up. Opportunity wasn't the problem. I was overwhelmed.

And somewhere beneath the noise and exhaustion, in a space I had never allowed myself before, a new question slipped in. Not the panic of "what now?" but something sharper, quieter:

What's next?

I didn't want another role. I wanted a reset. And through all that noise, a faint signal broke through. Not another company badge, but a different direction, one that might give me back something I'd lost somewhere along the corporate climb—the feeling that I could actually choose what came next.

That day at the gate, I finally did something I'd been avoiding. I opened YouTube, started searching, and let myself tumble down rabbit holes: What is AI? How could I use it not for the company, but for me? I'd been surrounded by these tools for years, but I'd never actually sat down and figured out what they could do for my life, not just my job.

CHAPTER 2

EVERYONE GOT THE MEMO BUT ME

The seeds had been planted that winter, months before I realized they were taking root. It started on a Saturday in New York, over espresso martinis at Starbucks Reserve.

My friends Roshiana and Jazz had visited for the weekend. They were newly engaged, and while Roshiana went off to look at wedding dresses with her family in Brooklyn, Jazz and I found ourselves at Starbucks, trying their espresso martini flight and letting the conversation stretch into the afternoon.

I'd asked him about his job in sales, what he actually did day to day. Jazz started explaining that he worked with the founders of software companies, describing how artificial intelligence was becoming the foundation of these businesses and why they depended so heavily on cloud platforms to run everything.

Then he mentioned something about having "AI agents."

I remember thinking: are these mini robots, like Rosie from The Jetsons?

"No," he laughed, "there are ways you can automate your workflow. Instead of doing something manually every time, you set things up so they happen automatically in the background."

I was curious, but skeptical. How could you trust something if you weren't doing it yourself, monitoring it, making sure it was actually good enough?

Jazz kept going, describing how founders were building entire businesses heavily dependent on AI—how, without it, they wouldn't be able to do what they were doing. They were using these new tools to solve problems not just for their own companies, but for their customers.

At first, I thought: What's he talking about? But as he gave concrete examples, I found myself physically leaning in. This was interesting. But how would I even begin? I wasn't an engineer. I didn't have the technical background Jazz had.

It sounded fascinating but still felt abstract—like someone describing a country I'd never visited but might want to see someday.

Then came my annual review a few weeks later. Among the usual feedback, my manager mentioned something that stuck: I needed to find "wins" using Google's internal AI tools—tangible examples of value I could point to in performance reviews. It wasn't criticism, just an expectation. Everyone was supposed to be exploring how AI could drive efficiencies in their role. I made the appropriate notes and filed them away as one more thing to figure out eventually.

But somewhere between Jazz's enthusiasm and my manager's expectations, I started noticing the conversations everywhere.

I found myself at Postino in Arizona, catching up with Nicole and Evelyn over Sancerre and shared plates. We'd all worked together in finance at Intel years ago, and they'd both moved on to new companies since then. I was on my way to Sacramento to meet baby Elle for the first time, and this dinner felt like a perfect pause in the middle of all the uncertainty about my future.

As we settled into our usual rhythm of catching up, I found myself talking through the Google situation—how I was leaning toward taking the severance instead of scrambling for another internal role, feeling both relieved and terrified about what came next. They listened with the kind of attention that only comes from people who've known you long enough to understand what a big deal this was.

"Have you thought about really leaning into AI?" Nicole asked, swirling her wine. "Not just for work, but for yourself?"

I probably made a face, because she kept going: "No, seriously. For interview prep, for exploring ideas. It can be helpful for that kind of thing."

"It's like having a research assistant who never gets tired," Evelyn added. "I've started using some AI tools at work, and it's especially helpful when you're trying to get up to speed on something new."

I nodded along, filing it away as one more thing I should probably look into eventually. But sitting there with two smart women I trusted, hearing them talk about AI like it was just another useful tool, planted something. Not urgency, exactly, but curiosity.

Walking out of Postino, I found myself thinking about how natural the whole conversation had felt. They were practical people who'd found something that worked. Maybe that was the key I'd been missing.

The Noise Gets Louder

Suddenly, AI was everywhere I looked.

At the dog park, I overheard two women debating whether AI-generated art was "real art." On the subway, a businessman was dictating into his phone: "*Write a professional email declining this meeting.*" At dinner parties, conversations inevitably turned to someone's latest AI experiment: a friend who'd used it to plan her entire European vacation, another who'd had it write his wedding toast.

A friend called from California to tell me he'd been using ChatGPT to help his son with homework. "It explains math better than I can," he laughed. "The kid gets it now."

Even Happy, my nail technician, had opinions. "I tried that ChatGPT thing," she said, filing my nails. "Asked it how to extend my business. Some ideas were actually pretty good. Wild, right?"

Colleagues started dropping AI acronyms in meetings like they'd been using them for years. "We should leverage LLMs for this." "Have you tried prompting it differently?" "The GPT output was surprisingly good." I'd throw in the occasional "mm-hmm," pretending I knew what they meant, while trying to decode this flood of acronyms I didn't recognize.

11

The local bookstore began featuring entire sections on "AI for Everyone." YouTube kept suggesting videos titled "I Tried AI for 30 Days and Here's What Happened" and "Why AI Will Change Everything (Or Destroy It All)."

LinkedIn became especially overwhelming. I'd check the app while walking Champ through the neighborhood, and it felt like everyone had transformed overnight into AI experts. Post after post scrolled by: "10 AI Tools That Will Transform Your Business." "How I Used ChatGPT to Land My Dream Job." "Why Your Company Will Fail Without an AI Strategy."

People I'd worked with for years were suddenly sharing screenshots of AI conversations like they were profound discoveries. A former colleague posted about using AI to write performance reviews. Someone from my MBA program shared how AI helped them prepare for board meetings. Even my old manager from Intel was posting about "leveraging machine learning for operational efficiency."

I'd scroll through this flood of AI success stories while Champ sniffed around his favorite fire hydrant, feeling like I was watching a party through a window. Everyone seemed to have figured out something I was missing. The comments were even more intimidating—dozens of people chiming in with their own AI wins, dropping acronyms I didn't recognize, casually mentioning tools I'd never heard of.

I'd put my phone away and focus on Champ, but that nagging feeling would follow me home.

The Overwhelm Sets In

I tried to catch up. I really did. I'd bookmark articles titled "A Beginner's Guide to Artificial Intelligence"—and never read them. I'd start watching explanatory videos, only to close them after two minutes when they dove into technical architecture and machine learning algorithms.

The problem wasn't just the technical jargon—though there was plenty of that. It was the speed. AI seemed to be moving so fast that by the time I wrapped my head around what ChatGPT was, everyone was already talking about GPT-5, Claude, Perplexity, and a dozen other tools I'd never heard of.

It felt impossible to catch up—like trying to jump onto a moving train that was accelerating every day.

Some days I'd feel motivated to learn. I'd open a new browser tab, search for "AI for beginners," and end up staring at explanations that assumed I already knew what terms like "large language models" and "neural networks" meant. I'd close the tab and get back to my day, slotting AI into the "someday, maybe" in my mental to-do list.

Other days, I'd get defensive. Maybe this was all hype. Maybe I didn't need to understand it. I'd been successful in tech for twenty years without it, right?

But that nagging voice kept getting louder, that familiar tightness in my chest growing stronger: What if I was missing something important? What if everyone else was figuring out something valuable while I sat on the sidelines, pretending I didn't care?

The Breaking Point

The breaking point came in April, during what was supposed to be a relaxing visit with my family in California.

I'd been staying with my brother Vince and Sandra for a few weeks, helping with baby Elle and trying to decompress from the chaos of job hunting. Elle was barely three weeks old then—all tiny fingers and that serious newborn frown that made her look like she was contemplating the mysteries of the universe. I'd hold her while she slept, marveling at how something so small could make everything else feel both more important and less urgent at the same time.

But even in that peaceful bubble, the noise followed me.

I'd sit on their couch with my laptop, Elle sleeping in my arms, scrolling through job listings while Champ stretched out at my feet and my brother's dogs, Belly and Sage, claimed their own spots nearby. Every posting seemed to mention AI somewhere:

"Familiarity with AI tools preferred." "Experience with machine learning is a plus." "Knowledge of LLMs and prompt engineering is desired."

I'd bookmark positions, then research the AI terms that appeared in job descriptions. What was prompt engineering? How "familiar" with AI tools did I need to be? I'd read articles about the future of work and AI, but found myself with more questions than clarity.

One evening, I met up with some former colleagues for dinner. I was looking forward to catching up, maybe getting their thoughts on the job market, and hearing about what they were working on.

Instead, the conversation quickly turned to AI.

"We've been experimenting with Copilot—it's like having an AI assistant built into Excel," one said. "It catches mistakes in our spreadsheets and saves us hours."

"I use ChatGPT for all my first drafts now," another chimed in. "Emails, project proposals, even meeting agendas. Then I edit from there. Saves me probably two hours a day."

"Have you tried any of the prompt engineering courses?" a third asked the group. "Basically, learning how to ask AI the right questions. There's some really advanced stuff you can do if you know how to structure your requests."

I sat there cutting my food into smaller and smaller pieces, piecing together what they meant. Courses on asking AI questions? I'd seen "prompt engineering" mentioned in job descriptions, but hearing people casually discuss taking actual classes on it made me realize how much I was still missing.

These were people I'd worked with for years. Smart, practical people who weren't usually early adopters of anything. And here they were, casually discussing AI tools like they'd been using them forever.

The conversation moved on, but I felt that familiar knot in my stomach growing tighter. Even here, trying to relax with old friends, I couldn't escape the reality that everyone had moved on to this new way of working while I was still trying to figure out the basics.

That night, lying in the guest room with Champ curled up beside me, I stared at the ceiling fan going around and around, feeling completely overwhelmed. Not just by the job search, but by the sense that the world had shifted while I wasn't paying attention—while I was working crazy hours for a job that wasn't going anywhere, only to be laid off anyway.

I thought about Elle, sleeping peacefully in the next room, and what kind of world she was going to grow up in. I thought about all the opportunities I might be missing because I was too intimidated to try.

I was tired of feeling left behind. Tired of being the person who stayed quiet while others discussed something that clearly mattered. Tired of closing browser tabs because the explanations assumed knowledge I didn't have.

Something had to change.

CHAPTER 3

HI, CHATGPT

So here I was, back at the Sacramento airport gate with Champ beside me after almost a month of job hunting, family time, and conversations that kept circling back to the same thing. Jazz is talking about AI changing everything. My former colleagues casually dropped terms I didn't understand. All those seeds planted over months were finally sprouting, ironically in spring, and I couldn't ignore them anymore.

Champ sensed my restless energy. He kept lifting his head to look at me, then settling back down with a small sigh, like he was saying, "Mom, you need to chill." But I couldn't shake the feeling that I was standing at some kind of crossroads.

The job search was fine, but not great. Some postings mentioned AI knowledge, though it wasn't universal. My former colleagues were casually using tools that felt foreign to me. And here I was, a woman who'd spent twenty years in tech, feeling like I was missing something everyone else had figured out.

That's when I finally pulled out my phone and opened YouTube. Not to watch dog videos but to search for something I'd been avoiding for months.

I typed: "What is AI?"

I scrolled through dozens of videos with intimidating titles like "Machine Learning Explained," "Neural Networks

17

for Beginners," and "The Mathematics Behind AI." My finger hovered over a few, but they all looked like they assumed I already knew what I was trying to learn.

Then I saw one that looked different: "AI Explained Like You're 5." The thumbnail showed a simple cartoon. No complex diagrams. No intimidating equations.

I put in my AirPods and pressed play.

A minute or two in, something clicked. The video broke it down with a simple shoelace example: traditional programming meant writing out every tiny step—"take the left lace, cross it over the right lace, pull it through"—like a recipe with hundreds of instructions for tying your shoes. But with AI, you could just show it lots of examples of tied and untied shoes, and it would figure out the pattern on its own. That made sense. AI wasn't following rigid instructions like traditional software. It was learning from examples, like a person would.

By the time we boarded the plane, I'd bookmarked half a dozen more videos to watch when I got home.

The Conversation That Changed Everything

It was past 7 AM when I finally got back to my Lower East Side apartment after the red-eye from Sacramento. I was exhausted but wired in that strange way you get when you've been traveling all night, too tired to sleep but too restless to sit still. Champ immediately claimed his spot on the ottoman, always needing time to decompress after flights, just like me. I sat staring at my laptop screen with my suitcase still by the door.

18

The apartment was quiet except for the street cleaner grinding by outside and the distant sound of early Manhattan traffic starting to build. It was that in-between hour when the city was waking up but hadn't quite started moving yet.

I'd used Gemini at work and for interview prep, and I'd even used ChatGPT, but I'd never really understood what I was actually working with. I'd been treating these tools like fancy search engines: ask a quick question, get an answer, move on. Something about the early hour, maybe mixed with the lingering effects of all those airport YouTube videos, made it feel safe to dig deeper this time. Like if I embarrassed myself, at least no one would be around to witness it. Just me, my jet-lagged brain, and whatever this AI thing actually was.

I opened a new browser tab and typed "ChatGPT." The page loaded with a simple white interface and a text box that said "Message ChatGPT."

I'd asked these tools basic questions before, but always felt like I was missing something fundamental. How do you actually have a real conversation with them?

Finally, I typed the only thing that felt natural: "Hi."

It responded immediately: "Hello! How can I help you today?"

Okay. That was... normal. Like texting with a very polite person.

I typed: "What is AI?"

What came back was a wall of text about machine learning algorithms, neural networks, and computational systems that can perform tasks typically requiring human intelligence. My eyes glazed over after the first sentence. It was like asking "What's for dinner?" and getting a dissertation on molecular gastronomy.

I was about to close the tab—this was exactly why I'd been avoiding diving deeper into this stuff—when I remembered something I often did in business meetings when concepts weren't clicking.

I tried again: "Help me understand this with an analogy?"

The Lightbulb Moment

What happened next changed everything.

Instead of more technical jargon, it gave me something I could actually picture: "Think of the difference between following a recipe and being an experienced chef. Traditional software is like following a recipe—like using a calculator where you type 2+2 and get 4, same result every time. AI is like an experienced chef who spent years studying thousands of recipes and cooking techniques, then uses all that knowledge to create something based on what you ask for."

I slowly leaned back in my chair, actually saying "huh" out loud. That made sense.

Traditional software gives you specific steps: type the numbers, press equals, and get the expected result every time.

But AI? You can ask it, "I want something warm and comforting," and it'll draw on everything it's learned—like how a chef knows the way garlic smells when it hits hot oil, how onions should smell when they're perfectly caramelized, what spices work together—to create something perfect for your request.

Traditional software is the recipe. AI is the chef.

For the first time, I understood what I'd actually been using when I opened Gemini at work. I wasn't drowning in acronyms and technical concepts anymore. I was having a conversation.

Digging Deeper

Emboldened, I kept going.

"What are LLMs? Everyone keeps mentioning them."

"If AI is like an experienced chef," it replied, "then an LLM—a Large Language Model—is like a chef who grew up studying every cookbook ever written, absorbing millions of recipes and techniques. They don't know everything perfectly, but they can recognize patterns, understand what you're asking for, and create responses that feel natural and helpful."

LLMs. The mysterious acronym had been floating around conversations for months. They weren't some incomprehensible technology—they were just the "chefs" who specialized in language, in having conversations.

ChatGPT, Claude, Gemini, Copilot—the names I'd been hearing everywhere—they were all LLMs. Different chefs with different specialties, but all trained on vast amounts of text to understand and respond to human language.

I asked one more question: "How is this different from Google search?"

The answer was simple but profound:

Search finds. AI explains.

21

Google search is like a librarian who runs to get you a book and points to page 32 where the answer is. An LLM is like a well-read friend who has already absorbed the book. They can explain the answer to you right now, in a way that makes sense for your specific question.

That distinction hit me like a lightning bolt. I'd been approaching AI like it was a fancy search engine, when it was actually something completely different. I wasn't searching anymore. I was having conversations.

The Bigger Picture

By the time nearly an hour had passed, something fundamental had shifted. I'd been intimidated by AI because I thought I needed to understand this massive, complex universe of technology.

But sitting there at 8 AM, with Champ now stretched out at my feet, I realized something liberating: I didn't need to understand the entire AI galaxy.

Here's what I wish someone had told me months ago: AI is like a vast galaxy with millions of different possibilities. AI shows up in more places than you might think. Some AI powers your smartphone camera to recognize faces in photos. Other AI figures out your Netflix recommendations or helps your phone predict what word you're typing next. There are AI systems that translate languages instantly, help doctors read X-rays, or power the voice assistant that dims your lights when you ask.

It's huge. It's complex. But you don't need to visit most of it.

Still, even as I was making sense of all this, I couldn't ignore the fact that AI leaves a footprint. Every prompt I type doesn't just appear out of thin air—it takes energy, and in many places, water, to keep the data centers running. For one person, the numbers sound tiny, maybe just a few drops here or a little electricity there. But scale changes everything. Billions of questions asked around the world add up.

I don't have all the answers here, and I'm not a sustainability expert. But I didn't want to write this book without at least acknowledging it. Exploring with AI isn't only about productivity or creativity. It also leaves a mark on the world we live in—and on the world my niece will grow up in.

The AI tools I was learning about—ChatGPT, Claude, Gemini, and others—they're all from just one solar system in this galaxy. The conversational corner. The place is designed specifically for people like me who want to ask questions in plain English and get helpful answers back.

The Path Forward

As I finally closed my laptop that morning, I felt something I hadn't experienced in months when it came to AI: genuine curiosity instead of overwhelming dread.

I wasn't behind anymore. I wasn't missing some crucial memo. I was simply at the beginning of learning to work with a new kind of tool—one that felt more like collaboration than following instructions.

Over the next few days, I found myself actually excited to continue experimenting.

Little did I know how spectacularly I was about to fail at almost everything I tried next.

CHAPTER 4

SPECTACULAR FAILURES

That excitement I felt after my breakthrough conversation with ChatGPT? It was intoxicating: it came with a dangerous side effect.

For the first time since getting laid off, I could see a path that didn't involve going back to what I'd always done. AI wasn't just interesting anymore; it felt like my ticket to building something completely different. Why return to the corporate playbook when I could write my own?

I was back in my Lower East Side apartment, officially "exploring my options" while Champ claimed his spot on the couch. The traditional job search felt like stepping backwards. More presentations about strategy. More meetings where I'd never make it into the room where decisions were made. I'd spent twenty years climbing that corporate ladder. Did I really want to start all over again at someone else's company?

But now? Now I had discovered something that could change the game entirely. AI wasn't just a conversational chef—it was my path to entrepreneurial freedom.

I had visions of creating content, automating tasks, and maybe even launching a business. The online videos made it look so easy: "Build a Million-Dollar App Using Only AI" and "Create 100 Videos in One Day with AI."

I was about to discover that understanding AI and actually building with it were two very different things.

How hard could it be? Famous last words.

Mr. Champ and Friends: A Masterpiece in the Making

My first project seemed perfect: an animated series starring my dog Champ. I'd call it "Mr. Champ and Friends," featuring his three best buddies from around the country. There was Nugget, my friend Shelley's French Bulldog, a goofball who needed to be carried home when he got tired on walks. Lola, my friend Nicole's brilliant Weimaraner, who could open doors and lock her brother Dexter in rooms just because she could. We'd recently lost her, and I loved the idea of her living on in these stories. And Bart, my friend Laura's pit bull, the sweetest, cuddliest thing you'd ever meet.

The whole thing would be perfect for my niece Elle to watch when she got older: wholesome, funny, featuring dogs she'd know and love, including one whose memory deserved to be celebrated.

I spent hours bouncing between different AI tools. I used ChatGPT to brainstorm story lines, then switched to Gemini because I thought it wrote better dialogue. Then came the hard part: turning those scripts into actual animations. I tried CapCut, Animaker, Pictory, and Adobe—all these different video tools that promised to make animation easy. These were from a completely different part of the AI world than the conversational tools I'd been using.

The results were... well, "disaster" would be generous.

The scripts read like they were written by a robot dog giving a formal speech about friendship. Sample dialogue: "Greetings, fellow canines. Today, we shall embark upon an adventure that will strengthen the bonds of our interpersonal relationships."

This was supposed to be a kids' show about dogs getting into mischief, not a corporate training video.

The animations were even worse. I'd spend three hours creating what the tools promised would be "professional-quality animation," only to get 8-10 seconds of footage that looked like it was made in 1995. In one version, Nugget's French Bulldog face melted halfway through like he was in a Salvador Dalí painting. I actually laughed out loud at how bad it was. Then felt frustrated that I'd spent three hours on ten seconds that looked terrible.

In another, all four dogs floated mysteriously above the ground like furry ghosts.

I kept telling myself, "Elle will love this," while looking at animations that would probably give her nightmares.

Go Fetch Ride: The "Expedia for Ride-Shares"

Undeterred by my animation failures, I moved on to my next brilliant idea: Go Fetch Ride, the "Expedia for ride-shares." The concept was simple: one app where you could compare prices across Uber, Lyft, and other services, then book the cheapest option.

27

An online video promised I could build it in 30 minutes using AI. Thirty minutes! I'd have my own startup by lunchtime.

Reality hit like a cold shower. Building an app requires technical connections to services like Uber and Lyft that aren't open to the public. You need something called APIs: basically, special permissions and technical bridges that let different apps talk to each other. You also need developer accounts, legal agreements, and about a dozen other things the online video conveniently forgot to mention.

I spent two days trying to figure out how to even get started before realizing I'd need a team of actual developers, months of negotiations with ride-share companies, and probably a few hundred thousand dollars in startup capital.

The 30-minute app? More like 30 months, if I were lucky.

The Children's Book Publishing Empire

My third spectacular failure was the most embarrassing. I'd watched countless videos promising I could use AI to write books, create covers, upload them to Amazon, and make $10,000 a month in passive income.

The process seemed foolproof. Ask AI to write a children's book. Design a cover. Upload to Amazon. Collect checks.

I followed their prompts step by step, feeding it character descriptions, plot points, and even moral lessons I wanted Elle to learn when she got older.

What came back was technically a children's book. It had a beginning, middle, and end. It had colorful descriptions and even some rhyming verses.

But it read like it was written by someone who had studied children's books through a manual rather than actually reading to kids. The dialogue felt forced. The adventures were generic. Every lesson was delivered with all the subtlety of a brick through a window.

The worst part? I could tell it was AI-generated from the first page. If I could spot it immediately, so could anyone else.

I never even got to the cover design or Amazon upload. I couldn't bring myself to put my name on something that felt so artificial, especially not something meant for Elle.

The Harsh Truth

After weeks of failures, I had to face reality: AI wasn't a magic wand. You couldn't just push buttons like a vending machine and get an animated series, a functioning app, or a bestselling book.

The less human involvement in these projects, the more obvious it became that they were AI-generated. Those online videos promising instant success? They were either overly optimistic or leaving out about 90% of the actual work required.

I felt like I'd been sold a dream that turned into a nightmare of melting dog faces and children's books that read like instruction manuals.

But somewhere in all that failure, I learned something important: AI wasn't the problem. My expectations were. I'd

29

been trying to use it as a replacement for human creativity and expertise, when what I really needed was to figure out how to work with it.

The breakthrough conversation I'd had with ChatGPT about AI analogies proved these tools could be genuinely helpful. The problem wasn't AI itself: it was that I'd been following the wrong guidance. I'd been trying to copy other people's shortcuts instead of learning the fundamentals.

If I were going to make this work, I needed to stop chasing magic formulas and start finding teachers who could actually teach.

CHAPTER 5

FINDING MY TEACHERS

After a few days of spectacular failures, I was sitting on my couch in my apartment, staring at my laptop screen and feeling like maybe I'd made a terrible mistake.

I'd thought AI was going to be my ticket out of the traditional job search—my way of generating income without having to go back to sitting behind someone else's desk. Instead of updating my resume and networking my way into another corporate role, I'd imagined myself creating children's books, building apps, and launching animated series. AI was supposed to be the shortcut to entrepreneurial freedom.

But the app idea crashed against technical walls I didn't even know existed. The children's books read like they were written by a robot giving a lecture on friendship. The animated series looked like something that would give kids nightmares instead of making them laugh.

Champ had retreated to his favorite hot-weather spot, stretched out on the cool bathroom tiles, and I was halfheartedly playing games on my phone while a 45-minute "Complete AI Beginner's Guide" droned on in the background. Halfway through the video, I realized I hadn't absorbed a single concept. My mind had completely checked out.

Sitting there, I started to wonder: maybe AI wasn't going to save me from having to find a corporate job. Maybe I wasn't cut out for this after all.

But something stubborn in me refused to quit completely.

The Pattern I Knew

Science never came easily to me. I repeated chemistry three times in high school before finally finding a teacher who could explain molecular structures in a way that clicked. But when I had really good teachers—the ones who could break down complex ideas and show me exactly how things worked—I didn't just learn enough to pass the exam. I understood the fundamentals.

This taught me early that failure doesn't equal inability: it just means there's a mismatch between how you learn and how you're being taught.

Over the years, I'd gotten pretty good at recognizing when I needed better guidance. Whether it was finding mentors at work, coaches for new skills, or just people who could explain things clearly, I'd learned that the right teacher makes all the difference.

The problem wasn't AI itself—I'd already had that breakthrough conversation with ChatGPT that proved these tools could be genuinely helpful. The problem was that I'd been following the wrong teachers. Time to use a skill I'd been developing my whole life.

The YouTube Rabbit Hole

I'd spent nights down rabbit holes, clicking on anything with a promising thumbnail. YouTube had become both my best friend and my worst enemy. The algorithm kept suggesting more and more AI videos, and I'd fallen into the trap of clicking on everything.

"Make $10K Per Month with AI!" Click. "Build an App in 10 Minutes!" Click. "AI Will Replace Your Job Unless You Do This!" Click.

Most of these videos fell into three categories: creators who talked too fast and assumed I already knew terms I'd never heard before; people who made wild promises but skipped the actual work; or videos that were just recycled content with misleading titles.

I'd start watching with genuine hope and end up more frustrated than before. It felt like being in school with teachers who either talked over my head or promised there would be no homework while secretly assigning a ten-page paper.

I looked down and realized I was playing a game on my phone instead of listening. The video was halfway finished, and I hadn't learned a single useful thing.

My breaking point came with that 45-minute video. I was on the couch with my laptop, and Champ had abandoned his usual spot next to me for the cool bathroom tiles—it was one of those sweltering New York days when even the dog knew better than to generate extra body heat. The video promised to be a "Complete AI Beginner's Guide," but twenty minutes in, they were talking about transformer architectures and neural networks.

33

That's when I developed my rule: If you can't explain something clearly and quickly with real examples, I'm out. Life's too short to waste on teachers who can't teach.

Enter Kevin Stratvert

Then YouTube's algorithm did something right for once. It suggested a video by someone named Kevin Stratvert with the simple title "How to Use ChatGPT (2025)."

Kevin looked like a regular guy—not someone trying to sell me a course or convince me to join his online community. Just someone sitting at his desk, ready to explain something clearly. Within the first two minutes, I knew this was different.

Instead of diving into technical concepts, Kevin introduced me to his fictional business: the Kevin Cookie Company. He showed me exactly what he was typing into ChatGPT: "Write a marketing email for my cookie business."

What came back was generic and vague—something about "freshly baked cookies just for you" with a random 10% discount that Kevin pointed out would kill their margins.

"This is somewhat vague and very generic," Kevin said, looking at the response. "Is that the fault of ChatGPT or is it the fault of my prompt?"

Then he showed me the magic. He tried again with a detailed prompt: "Write a fun and engaging marketing email for the Kevin Cookie Company. We have a new seasonal flavor, the pumpkin spice chocolate chip. Use playful language, offer a 5% discount, and keep it under 150 words."

The second response was completely different. It had personality, specific details, and the exact discount amount. It felt like something a real business would actually send.

"This shows how adding just a little bit of extra context and information to your prompt turns the output from something generic into a tailored and effective message," Kevin explained.

I stretched out on the couch with newfound confidence. For the first time in weeks, I understood something fundamental about working with AI. It wasn't magic—it was about being specific about what you wanted.

Kevin's videos were under 20 minutes, used concrete examples I could follow along with, and showed me his actual prompts. Most importantly, he didn't pretend AI was perfect. When something didn't work, he explained why and demonstrated how to adjust it.

I binged most of his YouTube playlist that evening, taking notes like I was back in college.

Jeff Su: The Google Connection

Kevin had shown me that AI teachers could be clear and practical, but I wanted to learn from someone who'd actually worked in my world. That's when I found Jeff Su.

The moment I saw "Former Googler" in his YouTube bio, I felt a spark of recognition. I didn't know him personally, but I felt like I knew him—I'd worked with people just like him for years. Here was someone who understood the corporate world I came from, who could speak the language of deadlines and deliverables.

35

When Jeff explained context in prompts, he used an example I immediately understood: imagine your vegetarian friend asks for restaurant recommendations. Of course, you wouldn't suggest a steakhouse, but AI doesn't know your friend is vegetarian unless you say so. The same is true at work—if you want help preparing for a raise negotiation, you need to spell out the details, not assume the AI already knows.

He paired that kind of everyday analogy with clear decision-making frameworks: "If you need a single fact, use Google search. If you need a fact with an explanation, use ChatGPT. If you need to analyze a large document, try Claude."

That simple framework cut through all the noise. It wasn't about chasing shiny new apps—it was about choosing the right tool for the job, the same way you'd decide whether something belongs in a text, email, or full report.

Hearing it from someone who'd navigated the same corporate environment I had felt like advice from a smart colleague who had already done the homework.

The Pattern Emerges

Between Kevin and Jeff, I started to see a pattern in the teachers who actually helped me learn – and suddenly, all those conversations where people casually mentioned "prompt engineering" started making sense:

- **They used real examples instead of abstract concepts.** Kevin's cookie company wasn't real, but the business problems he solved were genuine. Jeff showed actual work scenarios I recognized from my own career.

- **They showed their work.** I could see exactly what they typed, what results they got, and how they adjusted their approach when something didn't work perfectly.

- **They respected my time.** Twenty minutes or less, every time.

- **They acknowledged limitations.** They didn't pretend AI was magic—they showed me where it worked well and where it fell short.

Most importantly, **they taught principles, not just tricks.** Instead of "here's 50 AI prompts to copy," they taught me how to think about prompting so I could create my own. This was what my former colleagues had been talking about over dinner, not some mystical skill, but a learnable way of having better conversations with AI.

The Personal Tutor Method

Once I understood what made a good AI teacher, I started looking beyond YouTube for more structured learning. That's when I discovered something powerful about combining traditional education platforms with AI tools.

I already had a Masterclass membership, and in my search for more structured learning, I started exploring similar platforms. That's how I discovered BBC Maestro, another subscription-based learning platform. One course caught my eye immediately: Jo Malone's "Think Like an Entrepreneur." I'd been wearing her perfume for years and was fascinated by her business story, so with entrepreneurship on my mind, it felt like the perfect course to dive into. To really absorb the material, I came up with a system: I'd watch each section and take detailed notes, capturing the key concepts and examples that resonated with me.

After finishing a section, I'd share my notes with ChatGPT: "I just watched this video on entrepreneurship from Jo Malone's course. Here are my key takeaways. Can you help me create a study guide with practical applications and help me think through how these concepts apply to my own projects?"

What came back was like having a personal tutor who'd absorbed my notes. It organized the concepts into digestible sections, highlighted the most important points, and even suggested ways to apply what I'd learned to my own projects.

What really struck me was Jo's approach to sharing her journey—the wins and struggles alike, without the corporate polish I was used to. Twenty years in corporate America had trained me to share only the successes, to bury failures in lessons-learned documents that no one read. Even in job interviews, you were supposed to turn your "weaknesses" into strengths and make every failure sound like a strategic pivot.

But Jo talked about her experiences—including the difficult moments—like they were just part of building a business. It dawned on me that if I was really forging my own path with AI, stepping outside the corporate playbook entirely, maybe I needed to abandon that habit of hiding what didn't work.

She also talked about being more than just your brand, about you being a person first, even when your name is on the products. That resonated deeply as I was figuring out my own path forward. Maybe being authentic meant sharing the spectacular AI failures alongside the breakthrough moments.

This note-taking approach became my bridge between passive watching and active learning. I could turn comprehensive courses into personalized study guides and practice scenarios tailored to my specific goals. For someone like me who learns better through conversation and interaction, this was a game-changer.

The Blended Learning Approach

This taught me something important: the best learning happens when you combine multiple approaches. Kevin and Jeff gave me practical, accessible instruction. Structured courses provided expert depth. AI helped me process and personalize all that information.

None of these resources alone would have been enough. But together, they created a learning system that worked for how my brain actually processes information.

The Shift

With better teachers, everything changed. I stopped trying to learn AI from random videos and started being intentional about who I listened to. I unsubscribed from channels that promised miracles and focused on creators who delivered practical value.

I also stopped trying to learn everything at once. Kevin's cookie company examples taught me about customer service applications. Jeff's professional tips showed me workflow improvements. Jo Malone's stories taught me about authentic vulnerability in business. More importantly, it showed me how I could use AI to learn from any expert, not just AI teachers. I didn't need to understand every corner of the AI galaxy; I just needed good guides for the areas that mattered to me.

The failures from the previous month suddenly made sense. I hadn't been lacking ability—I'd just been following the wrong advice from the wrong teachers. With better guidance, I was ready to try again.

But more importantly, I now had something I'd never had before: a way to learn from the best minds in any field, on my own timeline, in my own way. Instead of being limited by what I could afford or access, I could capture expertise from anywhere – like Jo Malone's entrepreneurship insights – and use AI to turn it into actionable insights for whatever I was trying to build.

Those early AI failures—the melting dog animations, the impossible app ideas, the soulless children's books—they'd happened because I was trying to copy other people's homework instead of developing my own thinking. Now I understand that the real power wasn't in following someone else's blueprint for success. It was in learning how to think alongside AI, how to bring my own judgment and creativity to conversations that could help me build something authentic.

I thought I'd been looking for AI teachers, but I'd actually found something much more powerful: a collaborator that could help me learn anything from anyone, explore any idea, and think through problems I'd never tackled before.

But first, I needed to understand something that would tie everything together: I knew AI wasn't a search engine, but I hadn't figured out how to truly collaborate with it.

Time to learn how to have a real conversation.

CHAPTER 6

FROM SEARCH TO FRIENDSHIP

Within two or three weeks of finding my better teachers, I'd settled into a new rhythm. The spectacular failures felt like ancient history now—those hours and days spent trying to build apps and animate melting dog faces had taught me something valuable, even if they hadn't generated the income I'd hoped for.

By now, I was using AI conversationally without really thinking about it. I'd watch a Jo Malone course, take my detailed notes, then open ChatGPT: "Hey, I just watched this video on entrepreneurship. Here are my key takeaways. How can I apply these insights to my podcast idea?" It felt natural, like bouncing ideas off a colleague, exactly the kind of blended learning approach that had started clicking for me.

But something strange started happening. I'd come back from my morning walk with Champ—he'd head straight to his breakfast while I opened my laptop to start the day. ChatGPT would load with its usual prompt: "What can I help you with?" And I'd catch myself typing "Good morning" before diving into my question.

At first, I thought I was being ridiculous. Why was I saying hello to software? But then I realized—this wasn't that

42

different from my normal workday. For years, especially during the pandemic and since, most of my work has been from home, alone. I'd spend my days in video meetings or chatting with colleagues through Google Chat.

Whether I was messaging a teammate in Mexico about a deadline or asking a colleague in Sweden for feedback on a proposal, my brain was already wired for text-based conversations as a primary way of getting work done. I'd never just start a chat with a colleague by demanding, "I need XYZ." You'd say, "Good morning, hope your day is going well, need a favor," right?

So when ChatGPT started responding helpfully to my questions, my brain just... adapted. One more conversation window open, one more helpful colleague to bounce ideas off. The fact that this "colleague" happened to be an AI instead of a human in another city didn't feel like that big of a leap.

But there was something deeper happening that I didn't fully recognize at first. Going from working at Google— where I had colleagues to bounce ideas off every day—to figuring out what's next on my own could feel incredibly lonely. I was researching projects, exploring business ideas, and working through the journey of entrepreneurship, mostly by myself. Having this conversational partner suddenly made it feel less isolating and more collaborative.

Meet Reese

The personalization went even further when I upgraded to ChatGPT Pro for $20 a month. The paid version let me create different projects and customize how the AI responded, and somewhere along the way, I started calling it "Reese."

One syllable. Easy to say. I wanted something gender-neutral, something that felt relatable and communicative but still acknowledged this was software, not a person. More practically, it felt awkward to keep typing "Good morning, ChatGPT" every time I started a conversation—like referring to your friend by their full name whenever you talked to them.

"Morning, Reese. I need help thinking through this client proposal."

"Hey, Reese, can you help me brainstorm ideas for my friend's 50th birthday party?"

My friends discovered this when I mentioned something like "Reese and I were brainstorming" or "I collaborated with Reese on this project."

"Who's Reese?" they'd ask.

"That's my name for ChatGPT."

"Did you name your AI?" they'd say, half-joking, half-concerned.

"Yeah, of course I did," I'd respond, genuinely puzzled by their surprise.

But it made perfect sense to me. I was very aware it was software, not a person. But it didn't feel like just me by myself anymore.

What I didn't realize was that this shift—from treating AI like software to treating it like a thinking partner—was actually the key to getting better results. I just stumbled into it accidentally.

The Stanford Discovery

I thought I was just doing what felt natural until I stumbled across a YouTube video by Jeremy Utley, a Stanford professor who'd been studying how people collaborate with AI. The video was called "How Stanford Teaches AI-Powered Creativity in Just 13 Minutes," and it stopped me cold.

Here was a Stanford professor articulating exactly what I'd been doing intuitively, giving academic language to my instincts. Jeremy had discovered something fascinating: people who treated AI like a teammate got dramatically better results than those who treated it like a tool. The outperformers coached their AI, gave it feedback, and—this was the key—got it to ask them questions.

He said something that perfectly captured what I'd discovered: "The fundamental orientation a lot of people take towards AI is 'I'm the question asker, AI is the answer giver.' But if you think about AI like a teammate, you say, 'Hey, what are ten questions I should ask about this?'"

That was exactly what I'd been doing without realizing it. My conversations with Reese had evolved from search-like queries ("How many podcasts are in New York?") to actual collaboration ("I have this idea about creating a safe space for people to share their dating experiences in NYC. Help me think through how to create something like that.").

Jeremy had this great line that perfectly captured what I'd discovered: "The only correct answer to the question 'how do you use AI?' is 'I don't. I don't use AI. I work with it.'"

Hearing him say that felt like validation. I wasn't being ridiculous—I was on track, doing what I should be doing. Woohoo, go me.

The Evolution of My Prompting

Looking back, I could see how my approach had changed completely.

Early days (treating it like a search): "How do I start a podcast?" "What equipment do I need for recording?" "How much does podcast hosting cost?"

After the shift (treating it like collaboration): "I'm thinking about starting a podcast focused on dating stories in New York. What are some questions I should be asking myself before I get started?"

"I want to create something authentic, not another advice show. Help me think through the format—what are some ways to structure this that would feel genuine?"

"What am I not considering about this idea? What could go wrong, and how might I prepare for those challenges?"

The difference wasn't just in my phrasing. When Reese gave me responses that felt generic or off-target, I didn't dismiss them as a limitation of the technology. I gave it feedback like I would to a colleague: "That's not quite what I'm looking for. Let me explain what I mean differently."

Or better yet, I'd ask: "What do you need to know from me to give a better answer?"

The Coaching Relationship

What Jeremy's video helped me understand was that the best AI collaborations were actually two-way coaching relationships.

I'd coach Reese by giving it context, clarifying what I needed, and providing feedback when responses missed the mark.

But Reese coached me too, by asking clarifying questions that pushed my thinking further: "What's your primary goal with this project—building an audience or creating a community?" "What would success look like for you in six months?" "What assumptions are you making that might not be true?"

Some of these were questions I would have eventually asked myself, but others – like examining my underlying assumptions – weren't on my radar. Reese brought up both the obvious questions sooner and the blind-spot questions I might never have considered.

I started ending many of my prompts with "What questions should I be thinking about that I haven't asked yet?" It became my secret weapon for uncovering blind spots I didn't know I had.

The Mindset Shift

The conversation shift wasn't just about better results—though those came too. It was about changing my entire relationship with learning and problem-solving, and quietly rebuilding confidence I didn't realize I'd lost.

Instead of feeling like I needed to know all the right questions before I started, I learned to think out loud with a thinking partner who could help me discover what I didn't know. There was something liberating about being able to ask "dumb" questions without judgment.

Instead of treating AI interactions like transactions ("Give me X, Y, and Z"), they became explorations ("Let's figure this out together"). I wasn't afraid to admit when I was confused or needed to try a different approach.

Instead of getting frustrated when responses weren't perfect, I got curious about how to improve the collaboration. That shift from frustration to curiosity became everything – and each successful iteration reminded me that I could figure things out, even in unfamiliar territory.

This willingness to experiment, ask questions, and iterate without fear of failure was doing more than improving my AI conversations. It was restoring something I'd lost somewhere in the corporate world: the confidence that I could tackle problems I'd never faced before.

This shift prepared me for something I didn't see coming: my first real AI success. Not a spectacular failure or a half-working experiment, but something that actually solved a real problem in my life.

I was about to discover that when you work with AI instead of just using it, you can accomplish things you never thought possible.

CHAPTER 7

MY FIRST REAL WIN

A few days after learning to work with Reese instead of just using it, I got a call that would test everything I'd learned about AI collaboration.

I'd just started a new role as fractional COO for a political organization. The job had come through my friend Meaghan as I was leaving Google. What attracted me wasn't desperation—it was the mission. This was a chance to do something that mattered while I figured out my next move.

The organization was small, scrappy, and moving fast. Which is why, on a Wednesday afternoon, I found myself staring at a problem that made my stomach drop.

We needed a website. Not eventually, not next month—immediately. The board meeting was in less than 48 hours, and we had nothing to show potential donors except good intentions and our mission statement.

The Vendor Reality Check

My first instinct was to do what I'd always done in corporate roles: find the right expert and get professional help.

Someone on the board had given me one vendor to look into, and I found a couple more through my own searching. They were all really responsive people who showcased good work. These weren't bad vendors doing bad things—they had

49

their own workflow timelines, probably projects already lined up.

I reached out to all of them, explaining our timeline and basic needs. We needed a simple landing page where people could learn about our work and, more importantly, make donations. Nothing fancy—just professional, functional, and fast.

The responses that came back felt like a slap in the face.

"Nine days, minimum." "We could potentially rush this in twelve days." "Two weeks if we prioritize your project."

I sat in my apartment, staring at these emails on my laptop screen. Maybe in different circumstances, nine days or two weeks could work. But all I kept thinking was: *I don't have that time.* It's Wednesday. The board meeting is on Friday morning.

I was relatively new to the organization. They hadn't set explicit expectations, but it was clear to me that I couldn't let a week go by and walk in with nothing. Maybe some of that was legacy corporate America thinking—you provide updates, you show results.

But beyond that, I knew having a website was crucial. We were an independent expenditure committee, which meant a big part of our mission was generating funds to support our cause. Without a website, we weren't getting money in the door. People would have to write actual checks. There was nothing on the internet for people to find us, to understand what we were about.

The Internal Pressure

The board wasn't expecting a website—I was expecting it of myself. But that pressure felt crushing.

Part of me worried about my reputation. Could I still deliver results after leaving Google? This wasn't just about building a website; it was about proving I belonged in this new world of consulting and fractional work.

Every day without a donation page was potentially lost funding. Every day we looked unprofessional was a day donors might choose other organizations to support.

I had two choices: pay someone extra to rush the job and hope they could meet the timeline, or try something I'd never attempted before.

In my old corporate playbook, the answer would have been clear—hire an expert and pay for speed. But what if I needed a different playbook?

The "Screw It" Moment

Here's the thing about me: if I can't find someone to do something for me, I'll figure it out myself. That's always been my approach—an extension of all those DIY projects around my home.

Sitting there looking at those vendor timelines, the leap didn't feel that big. *Screw it. I'm doing this myself.*

I couldn't walk into Friday's board meeting with nothing to show but vendor quotes and apologies about timelines.

The Partnership Moment

That afternoon, I did something that would have seemed impossible just weeks earlier. Instead of frantically googling "how to build a website in 24 hours," I opened my conversation with Reese.

"I'm a fractional COO of a political organization in New York City," I typed, "and I have less than 48 hours to get a website live. I've reached out to several vendors, and none of them can meet the timeline. What can we do together to come up with a plan?"

What came back wasn't a generic list of website builders or a lecture about realistic timelines. It was an actual conversation about solving a real problem.

"Let's break this down," Reese responded. "What exactly do you need this website to accomplish? What are the must-haves versus nice-to-haves? And what resources do you have available?"

Wait—this felt different. Not like searching for answers, but like brainstorming with a colleague who actually wanted to understand the problem.

For the next hour, we talked through the project like two people figuring out solutions together. Reese helped me understand the difference between a domain (your website's address, like 123 Main Street—no one else can have that address) and hosting (where the website actually lives).

When I got confused about technical terms, I didn't feel embarrassed to ask. "I don't understand what you mean by DNS settings," I'd type, and Reese would explain it using analogies I could grasp.

The frustrating part? Reese couldn't see my screen, so I had to screenshot everything. "Here's what I like about this site, here's what I don't like." And ChatGPT's memory isn't always great, so sometimes I had to repeat myself. But eventually, we figured out what I wanted.

The 24-Hour Sprint

What followed was the most intense learning experience of my life.

I had to do research first—looking at other political organizations' websites, taking screenshots of ones that worked, and ones that didn't. What colors felt trustworthy versus jarring? What kind of content did they include? Did they use multiple pages or keep everything on one scrolling page?

My thinking was: if people are already on our website, we've almost got them. Let's not make it complicated. Let's make it easy—here's who we are, here's our mission, here's what we're doing, and here's how you can donate and contact us. Short, sweet, to the point.

Reese guided me through every step: buying the domain (I'd done this before but understood the purpose better now), choosing between a hosting site, Squarespace or Wix, and selecting a template that looked professional but wasn't too complex.

When I got stuck—and I got stuck constantly—I'd share screenshots and ask for help.

"I'm looking at this page and it says 'SSL certificate pending'—what does that mean and should I be worried?"

53

"The donation button isn't working when I test it. Here's what I see when I click it—help me figure out what's wrong."

It was like having a patient colleague available 24/7. Someone who never got frustrated when I asked the same question three different ways, who could explain complex concepts using simple comparisons.

The breakthrough moment came when I realized I wasn't just following step-by-step instructions anymore. I was actually starting to understand how the pieces fit together. When something went wrong—and plenty did—I could troubleshoot it myself because I finally understood the logic behind it.

Friday Morning Reveal

Friday morning, I joined the board meeting on video, carrying more confidence than I'd felt in months.

After we went through the usual minutes from the prior week, the board chair asked if I had any updates.

"So I reached out to some vendors about the website," I started. "The timelines just didn't fit—some were quoting nine days, ten days, twelve to fourteen days. The prices varied, too, and I know we're trying to keep costs lean." I paused, sharing my screen. "So I took the liberty of building the website myself. Let me walk you through it. I'm open to feedback."

I shared my screen to show them a password-protected website that looked like it had been built by a professional team. Clean design. Clear messaging. Working donation forms. Contact information. Everything they needed and more.

The video call went quiet for a moment. I think they were surprised because they knew my experience wasn't in this space.

"This is exactly what we need," the board chair said as I walked through the landing page. "How quickly can we make it live?"

That's when I took the liberty of doing something I hadn't planned. "We can launch it right now," I said, and changed the website from password-protected to public while they all watched through the screen share.

The validation I felt wasn't just about the website—it was proof that I could still deliver, that I belonged in this new world I was building.

After that call ended, I did an emotional victory lap around my apartment. That felt freaking good.

What I'd Actually Learned

Looking back, the website itself wasn't the real accomplishment. What mattered was discovering that I could tackle something completely outside my expertise and figure it out in real-time.

I learned really quickly that it wasn't easy. I had to understand GoDaddy and Namecheap, figure out that buying a domain was just getting an address, then actually build something to live at that address. The templates weren't the easiest for me to use because I'm not naturally creative, so it took time to figure out what I actually wanted.

But I hadn't just built a website. I had built a new relationship with learning itself. Instead of feeling paralyzed by what I didn't know, I had gotten comfortable thinking out loud with a collaborator who could fill in the gaps.

The website launched successfully and served the organization well for months. But more importantly, I had proven to myself that the conversational approach to AI wasn't just a nice-to-have. It was a genuine competitive advantage.

When everyone else was waiting for experts to become available, I had learned to become my own expert, one question at a time.

That confidence would serve me well, because I was about to learn that I can accomplish things I never thought possible - even if it starts with something as simple as losing someone's phone number.

CHAPTER 8

THE NETWORKING NINJA'S PROBLEM

By early July, I was riding high from the website win. I had proven to myself and the board that I could tackle technical challenges I had never faced before. The confidence from that success was still fresh when I ran into a problem that was both more personal and more frustrating.

I kept losing people's phone numbers. Which sounds like such a basic problem, but these weren't random networking contacts—these were people who'd been vulnerable with me, who'd shared stories they rarely told, who'd offered to be part of something I was trying to build

The Podcast Foundation

My friends have always called me the "networking ninja." Not because I am aggressive about it, but because I seem to attract stories. Strangers tell me things on subway rides. People open up at dinner parties. My friend Cathy says I am "huggable," which is ironic since I am not particularly fond of hugs, but apparently, I give off something that invites people in.

This wasn't a new pattern. When I lived in California, I hosted Thanksgiving and Easter for people who were far from family or wanted a different kind of celebration. In Arizona, I

57

organized monthly wine and cheese nights, bringing together women from work, church, local meetups, and my neighborhood. I loved creating spaces where people could connect across different circles of their lives.

Living in New York, I found myself constantly hearing fascinating dating stories. Friends would share their latest adventures over dinner. Sometimes you'd witness awkward first dates at neighboring tables or overhear conversations on the subway, people opening up about their experiences in this overwhelming city.

There was something about New York that made people want to tell their stories, and I found myself thinking: what if there were a space designed specifically for these authentic experiences?

I called it The Dating Mosaic. The idea was that every person's story was like a unique tile, and together they would create something beautiful and complex. I wasn't trying to give dating advice or solve anyone's problems. I just wanted to create a safe space where people could share their real experiences—the messy, beautiful, complicated reality of looking for love in one of the world's most overwhelming cities.

For someone who'd spent years creating spaces for authentic connection, a podcast felt like a natural evolution. Same instinct, different medium.

The Vanishing Contacts

As the project developed, I hit a breaking point that had nothing to do with technology and everything to do with my own disorganization.

I'd been meeting incredible people with powerful stories. A woman who approached me after overhearing my podcast ideas at a friend's dinner party. She normally wouldn't share personal details with strangers, but she said she had a beautiful story she wanted to tell about finding love where she'd least expected it.

Then there was a gentleman I met at a cafe, a widower who'd been married for thirty years. His wife had passed away two years earlier, and he wanted to talk about what it meant to think about love again after such a profound loss.

Both had been vulnerable with me in that generous way people are when they sense someone truly listening. Both had offered to be part of the podcast when I was ready to start recording.

And I lost both their contacts.

The woman's number was somewhere in my phone's 800+ contacts, saved under who knows what name. The widower had given me his business card after we met at the cafe, but it vanished during a busy week. I thought I'd put it in my wallet—checked there first. Nothing. Then I flipped through my journal, where I usually tuck important things. Not there either. I even tried to remember what I was wearing that day, checking the pockets of my clothes hanging in my closet. No luck. The frustration hit me like a wave.

These weren't just networking connections. These were people who'd trusted me with parts of their story. Losing their information felt like betraying that trust.

But there was a deeper fear lurking underneath my frustration: if I couldn't keep track of potential guests, what chance did I have at actually creating this podcast and making it successful? The disorganization wasn't just embarrassing—it was undermining the entire project before it even began.

The QR Code Solution

Sitting in my apartment that evening, frustrated with myself and listening to the sounds of the city settling into the night, I opened my conversation with Reese.

"I meet people at events who want to be on the podcast," I typed. "I need a simple way for them to share their information so I don't lose it. What can we do together to solve this?"

What followed was my first real collaborative problem-solving session since the website. Not a crisis with a forty-eight-hour deadline, but a practical challenge that needed an elegant solution.

"Let's think through this step by step," Reese responded. "What happens from the moment someone says 'I'd love to be on your podcast' to when you actually need to contact them?"

We mapped out the entire workflow: the initial conversation, exchanging contact information, my phone getting buried in my purse, information getting lost in the shuffle of daily life, and my inevitable frustration days later when I couldn't find their details.

"What if we created a system that worked even when you're distracted or in a hurry?" Reese suggested. "Something people could access immediately while they're still thinking about it?"

That's when we landed on the QR code solution.

Building the System

I thought this would take ten minutes. Two hours later, I was still at my laptop, talking myself through each step. "Okay, why isn't this connecting?" I kept saying out loud, while Champ just looked at me like, "Mom, you're talking to yourself again."

But it was two hours of learning that felt like unlocking a superpower.

The biggest surprise wasn't the technical complexity—it was realizing how many small decisions went into something that seemed simple. Should the form ask for their story up front or just basic contact info? How personal should the automated thank-you email sound? What if someone made a typo in their email address?

Each choice forced me to think through the actual experience I wanted to create, not just the mechanics of collecting information.

Reese walked me through creating a QR code - one of those square barcodes people can scan with their phone camera. But instead of just linking to a contact form, we built something smarter.

When people scanned the code, they'd go to a simple web page where they could enter their information, tell me a bit about their story, and indicate their interest in being a guest. That information would automatically feed into a spreadsheet I could access from anywhere. Even better, it would trigger a thank-you email letting them know I'd received their information and would be in touch soon.

Reese guided me through each step, but it didn't magically do the work for me. I still had to make decisions about design, write the text, and test everything to make sure it worked. Reese was the patient guide, but I was still the one building the solution.

The Test

When I tested the system with a few friends, it actually worked. Someone could scan the code with their phone, fill out the quick form, and within minutes, I had their information organized while they received a personal email from me.

I spun around in my chair to tell Champ, who was stretched out on his favorite spot on the couch. "It works!" He lifted his head, gave me that look he gets when I'm being dramatic about something he doesn't understand, then went right back to sleep. Like, "Great job, Mom. Can I nap now?"

That tiny win opened my eyes. Not because the solution was revolutionary, but because I'd identified a real problem in my life and built a system to solve it. I was using our collaboration to improve something that mattered to me.

The Real Victory

The QR code system worked beautifully, helping me connect with dozens of potential guests without losing a single contact. But the real victory was recognizing that I didn't need to wait for someone else to build solutions for my problems.

I could identify what wasn't working, think through better approaches, and build systems that fit my specific needs and workflow. AI wasn't replacing my judgment or creativity. It was amplifying my ability to turn ideas into reality.

Little did I know that this small victory was building something bigger than a contact system—it was building my confidence that I could identify what wasn't working in my life and actually do something about it. Instead of just scrambling to fix problems after they happened, I was learning to build systems that prevented them in the first place.

63

CHAPTER 9

LOSING THE PLAYBOOK

The success with the QR code system should have felt like a victory lap. I had identified a real problem, built a working solution, and proven I could tackle technical challenges that would have intimidated me months earlier. I thought this meant I'd finally 'figured out' AI—that I now had the secret to working with these tools effectively.

Except I didn't feel consistently confident. I felt lucky.

Two successful projects didn't feel like mastery—it felt like I'd stumbled onto something that worked, but I had no idea if I could do it again. So naturally, I went looking for the formula that would make it repeatable.

The Template Trap

I don't even remember what podcast problem I was trying to solve that evening. What I do remember is looking up from my laptop around 11 PM, exhausted, and realizing I had fifteen browser tabs open—all different AI videos promising to fix whatever I'd been struggling with.

Champ was asleep in his bed, and I was sitting there thinking, 'What the hell am I doing?' My desk was a disaster—notes scattered everywhere, half-watched tutorials, conflicting advice from people who all claimed to have the answer.

There wasn't a specific moment that broke me. I was just tired. Tired of searching for the magic formula when what I really needed was probably right in front of me.

The Homework Problem

The real issue wasn't with Kevin and Jeff. They were still the best teachers I had found. Kevin's approach of using concrete examples was brilliant. Jeff's frameworks for choosing between different AI tools were exactly what I needed to understand.

The problem was that I had been trying to copy their homework instead of learning from their teaching methods.

When Kevin showed how to use ChatGPT for customer service at his fictional cookie company, I tried to replicate his exact scenario instead of applying his principle—use specific, realistic examples—to my own projects. When Jeff demonstrated his decision-making framework with his work situations, I copied his prompts word-for-word instead of adapting his strategic thinking to my own challenges.

I was like a student who copied another student's math homework instead of learning how to solve the equations. I could reproduce their exact steps, but I couldn't tackle new problems on my own consistently.

The Revelation

That evening of frustration led to a realization that changed my thinking: I needed to stop copying my teachers' homework and start applying their lessons to my own work.

Kevin had taught me to use concrete examples and show my work. But instead of creating examples relevant to my podcast and consulting projects, I was trying to force cookie company scenarios into situations where they didn't fit.

Jeff had taught me to think strategically about when to use different tools. But instead of developing my own decision-making process based on his principles, I was copying his exact prompts for completely different situations that had nothing to do with mine.

The breakthrough came when I looked back at my actual successes—the website, the QR code system, even that first helpful conversation about AI analogies. None of those had followed anyone else's templates. At the time, I'd just been scrambling to solve urgent problems with whatever resources I had. But looking back, I could see they all shared something: I'd brought my own context and judgment to the conversation, working with AI in my natural problem-solving style rather than trying to force myself into someone else's system.

Finding My Own Voice

The next morning, I woke up and did something that felt both obvious and radical. I opened my laptop and started deleting files. All those 'proven prompts' I'd collected? Gone. The template libraries I'd been hoarding like they were treasure? Deleted. It felt like cleaning out a closet full of clothes that never fit right.

What I finally started organizing was an approach that looked nothing like the systems I had been trying to copy. But it felt completely authentic to how I actually thought and worked.

I already knew I liked starting conversations with context about what I was trying to accomplish, not just jumping into requests. I'd learned I preferred collaborative back-and-forth over single-shot prompts. I'd seen that I got better results when I treated AI like a thinking partner rather than a sophisticated search engine.

Instead of forcing myself into other people's templates, I was finally putting these pieces together in a way that made sense for me – thinking out loud and letting conversations develop naturally.

Most importantly, I was connecting what I'd discovered: my best collaborations happened when I brought my own expertise and judgment to the conversation, rather than trying to let AI do the thinking for me.

The Pattern Recognition

As I gradually stopped forcing myself into other people's molds, something interesting started happening. I'd catch myself mid-conversation with Reese thinking, 'Wait, this actually feels natural.' Looking back at what was working, I started seeing patterns I'd been blind to before:

I did better when I explained not just what I wanted, but why I wanted it and what constraints I was working within.

I got more useful responses when I asked AI to help me think through problems rather than just demanding solutions.

I preferred working iteratively—starting with rough ideas and refining them together—rather than trying to craft perfect prompts on the first try.

I found that all those years of figuring things out in corporate environments—breaking down problems, working with different personalities, finding solutions when there wasn't an obvious playbook—were actually an asset, not something I needed to overcome. The same instincts that had helped me succeed at Google and Intel were exactly what made me effective at working with AI. Whether you've spent years in corporate settings, creative fields, or figuring things out on your own, those problem-solving instincts you've developed are probably more relevant than you think.

Permission To Be Myself

The most important shift wasn't technical. It was psychological. I finally stopped feeling like I was behind or doing it wrong. I stopped apologizing for not being a "natural" at AI or feeling embarrassed when my approach didn't match what I saw in videos. Maybe you're feeling that same pressure to do it 'right,' or maybe you're just trying to figure out where to start – either way, there's probably more room for your authentic approach than you realize.

Instead, I started trusting that my twenty years of experience solving problems, managing projects, and working with different types of people had actually prepared me well for this new type of collaboration.

I didn't need to become someone else to be good at AI. I just needed to figure out how to bring my existing strengths to these new conversations.

The New Foundation

By the end of that week, I felt like I was standing on completely different ground. Instead of constantly looking over my shoulder at what other people were doing, I was looking ahead at what I wanted to accomplish.

I wasn't trying to become an AI expert who could impress people with technical knowledge. I was becoming someone who could use these tools effectively to solve real problems and build things that mattered to me.

The website, the QR code system, and the collaborative conversations—they all connected now. They had worked because I had approached them authentically, bringing my own perspective and judgment to collaborative problem-solving.

I was ready to stop trying to master other people's systems and start building my own approach. The playbook I'd been searching for didn't exist—because I needed to write it myself. The question was no longer, "What's the right way to use AI?" but, "How can I work with AI in a way that strengthens who I already am?"

That shift would prove crucial, because I was about to discover that the real power of AI wasn't in following perfect formulas. It was in building systems that worked specifically for me.

69

CHAPTER 10

FIVE FRIENDS, FIVE TOOLS

Having my own approach figured out was one thing. Organizing my daily work was another.

By the time I'd stopped following other people's playbooks, I realized I needed a roadmap of my own. Without one, I was still trying things at random—sometimes hitting gold, sometimes wasting hours. The breakthroughs came when I started grouping my AI use into different types of help.

Suddenly, instead of asking "What can this thing do?" I was asking, "What kind of help do I actually need right now?"

After weeks of jumping from tool to tool, trying everything and mastering nothing, I started noticing patterns. Some tools kept showing up in 'research' tutorials. Others seemed designed for creative brainstorming. What had felt like complete chaos slowly started organizing itself into five clear categories.

But which tools actually worked for which categories? I'd been treating all AI assistants like they were the same, but that's like saying all restaurants serve the same food. Through trial and error, I started to see their personalities.

Each one served a different purpose and required me to think about it differently. Once I could name them, I could use them on purpose instead of just hoping for the best.

As I developed these categories, I realized they reminded me of something I already knew: the different strengths of my friends. We all have that one person who's the natural researcher, the wordsmith, the organizer. AI was like having access to all those different types of help in one place.

When I'm Starting from Zero

This is my friend Nicole. If I tell her I'm looking for a new suitcase, she'll disappear into online research, then come back with three perfect options complete with pros, cons, and price comparisons. She loves digging into topics just for the satisfaction of understanding them.

For research, I found Claude was like Nicole at her most patient—he explained complex topics clearly without making me feel lost for asking basic questions. ChatGPT/Reese was faster for quick definitions, while Gemini worked seamlessly with Google tools I was already using. Each had their research personality. Perplexity became my fact-checking companion when I needed not just an explanation but also sources to verify information. It would search the web and cite where it found each piece of information.

Reese became my research helper the same way—not the final word, but the first step. Quick explanations, comparisons, and simple introductions to topics that were new to me. Instead of starting with a blank Google search, I could start with some basic understanding.

71

I can't count the number of times I've asked Reese something like, "Explain the difference between these two types of business insurance," or "What does this technical term actually mean?" It wasn't like I suddenly became an expert, but at least I could bridge the knowledge gap and start asking the kinds of questions that actually moved conversations forward.

Did I still need to double-check with real experts? Of course. But the difference between starting at zero and starting with some knowledge is huge.

While I was working with the political organization and people started using complex terms, I'd go to Reese first, get the basic understanding, then ask informed questions that kept discussions productive instead of slowing them down.

This taught me to think of Reese as my quick primer—just enough to get me started, never the final word.

When I Need Help Getting My Words Right

This reminds me of my friend Marquette. She has this gift for taking messy ideas and turning them into clear, compelling writing. She can take your scattered thoughts and hand them back to you, polished but still in your voice.

ChatGPT became my Marquette—great at conversational writing and helping me find different ways to say things. Claude was better at longer, more structured pieces that needed logical flow. Both helped me write faster without losing my voice.

At first, I thought AI writing meant letting it "do it for me." Wrong. The real power came in treating it like a writing partner. Helping with drafts, suggesting different ways to say things, and tightening up my copy. I wasn't giving up my voice. I was making it sharper.

One of my early wins came with campaign materials. I had to write creative briefs that needed to be tight, persuasive, and follow legal rules. Instead of staring at a blank screen, I shared my rough outline and asked ChatGPT to suggest three different ways to structure it.

From there, I picked the best pieces, added my own words, and worked on it until what felt overwhelming became manageable.

This wasn't about being lazy. It was about moving faster. I could go from nothing to a decent first draft—leaving my energy for editing and polishing where my voice mattered most.

When I was writing documents for my consulting work, I'd start with my rough thoughts and let ChatGPT help me organize them more clearly. But the final version always had to sound like me, represent my values, and reflect my actual experience. AI gave me the structure. I built the content.

When I Need to Get Organized and Save Time

Think of my friend Suhas. He's the one who sets up systems that just work. While the rest of us are manually doing the same task over and over, he's quietly creating shortcuts that handle it automatically. He sees patterns and time-wasters that the rest of us miss.

For automation and organization, I found myself gravitating toward tools that could connect with other apps I already used. Some AI assistants were better at understanding workflows, while others excelled at creating reminders and follow-ups. The key was finding ones that worked with my existing habits rather than forcing me to adopt completely new systems.

This category surprised me the most. AI isn't just about conversations—it can handle the behind-the-scenes work. Sending thank-you emails to podcast guests automatically. Organizing information. Creating reminders. This shifted me from just using AI to actually building helpful systems with it.

Airtable became my go-to for this; think of it as a smart spreadsheet that can also automate tasks and send reminders. It helps me track what I'm working on, tasks, deadlines, and experiments, so AI doesn't just live in our chat conversations. It becomes part of a system I can actually manage.

The clearest example? Guest follow-up for The Dating Mosaic. Before, I was manually checking lists, writing notes, and sending follow-ups. Now I have a system that creates thank-you messages and keeps track of everything automatically. The system works while I sleep.

When my friend Brandon told me about his restaurant reporting problems, I walked him through this same approach. As a manager, any time there's an incident during his shift – equipment issues, customer complaints, staff problems – he has to fill out detailed incident reports using the restaurant's template. After an exhausting shift, sitting down to remember and document everything that happened was brutal.

Now he records quick voice notes on his phone as things happen or right after incidents occur. At the end of his shift, he takes those voice transcripts, feeds them into AI, and asks it to organize the information using the restaurant's report template. Instead of spending thirty minutes trying to remember details and fill out forms, he spends five minutes editing the reports that captured everything accurately. The information gets documented properly, and he gets home to his family faster.

This type of AI help is invisible but powerful. No one sees it, but it's the difference between drowning in paperwork and creating space for what actually matters.

When I Want to Try New Ideas

This is pure Luiza energy. She's the friend who sees possibilities everywhere, who can take a small idea and spin it into ten different creative directions. She's always experimenting, always asking "what if we tried this instead?"

For creative brainstorming, different tools had different energy levels. ChatGPT was like Luiza on caffeine—endless enthusiasm and wild ideas. Claude was more thoughtful, helping me develop concepts more systematically. Midjourney and DALL-E let me visualize ideas that were hard to describe in words. Gamma helped me quickly turn concepts into polished presentations. I learned to match the tool's creative style to what kind of brainstorming I needed.

Here's where the fun lives. Video ideas, project concepts, creative experiments. Sometimes it's messy, sometimes it's magic. Creative work with AI doesn't replace imagination. It speeds it up. It's where "what if?" turns into "let's try this."

Take The Dating Mosaic. I start with guest ideas—short conversations, story pieces, potential directions. Then I share those with Reese to help me brainstorm episode themes, titles, and angles. From there, I ask it to spin out concepts, snippets, even rough video ideas. Some were throwaway ideas. But others had enough spark to build an entire episode around.

The key is staying in control of the creative process. AI can generate a hundred ideas, but I decide which ones match my vision and values. It's like having an enthusiastic helper with endless energy—you can give it a hundred different starting points, and it never gets tired of brainstorming. The trick is knowing when to say yes to the help and when to say no. Sometimes that means recognizing when AI-generated content would contradict what you're trying to build. Never let it replace your authentic voice.

When I Need to Think Through Big Decisions

This is my friend Rose. She can see around corners in ways that constantly surprise me. While I'm focused on the immediate challenge, she's asking, 'Have you thought about what this looks like six months from now?' or 'What could go wrong that we're not seeing?' The kind of strategic questions that completely re-frame how you approach a problem.

For strategic thinking, I needed tools that could handle complexity without getting lost in details. Claude became my go-to for this kind of work—it could hold multiple variables in mind and help me think through scenarios. ChatGPT was good for quick strategic checks, but for deep planning, I needed something that could think as systematically as Rose.

This is where it gets most interesting —where I use AI to think alongside me, not just work for me. Planning for different scenarios, developing frameworks, and testing ideas before they meet the real world. This is where curiosity, practice, and experience all come together.

I've used it for political work, exploring scenarios to understand which areas of New York might respond differently to different approaches. Instead of locking myself in a room with spreadsheets, I could ask questions like: "If we focus on this neighborhood instead of that one, what might happen?" AI wouldn't give final answers, but it would suggest frameworks, trade-offs, and questions I hadn't considered.

When clients approach me with projects in industries I've never worked in—beverage distribution, consumer products, nonprofit fundraising—I use this approach to get up to speed quickly. Perplexity helps me gather current industry data and recent developments that inform the strategic questions I need to ask. Not to become an expert overnight, but to ask good questions and understand the landscape well enough to add real value.

This is where I stopped seeing AI as just a helpful tool and started seeing it as a thinking partner. Not the decision-maker, but the sparring partner that sharpens your thinking.

Making Sense of It All

Looking back, this roadmap wasn't obvious at the start. It only emerged after plenty of trial and error. But once I had it, I stopped feeling overwhelmed by all the possibilities.

Every new tool, every new experiment had a place. I could learn faster and build confidence step by step.

The categories also helped me explain my work to others. When people asked how I'd built my consulting website, I could walk them through the specific types of help I'd used: research to understand web development basics, organization to handle the technical setup automatically, creativity to develop the content, and strategic thinking to figure out my positioning.

Instead of magic, it was a method.

That's the gift of having categories. They don't limit you—they free you. Because once you know the different types of help available, you get to decide what you need. And when new AI tools come out—which they will, constantly— you're not starting from scratch.

You're asking: "What type of help does this provide? How does it compare to what I already use? Is it worth the time to learn?"

My approach gave me principles for how to work with AI. The categories gave me a structure for organizing that work. But I still needed one more piece to make it sustainable: boundaries that would keep me from losing myself in the process.

CHAPTER 11

CONTEXT IS EVERYTHING

Having categories was like finally organizing that junk drawer everyone pretends they don't have. I knew where everything was, but that didn't mean I knew what to do with it. I was about to learn the hard way that knowing what AI could do was completely different from knowing how to make it actually useful.

The shift happened during one of those exhausting New York days when nothing was going right. I was meeting a friend for dinner, running late (as usual), and realized I had no idea where we were eating.

My first instinct was to ask Reese: "Good restaurant in Union Square?"

Generic list. Twenty places. Half of them are tourist traps. Useless.

I sat there on the subway, annoyed at myself. This was becoming a pattern—AI giving me technically correct but completely unhelpful answers. Then something clicked. Wait. I wasn't talking to a search engine like Google. I was supposed to be having a conversation.

So, I tried again: "I need a restaurant in Union Square, within 10 minutes of the subway, good for catching up with a friend who just went through a breakup, somewhere we can actually hear each other talk, preferably with good wine because we're going to need it."

Three perfect options came back. Not twenty. Three. And they were exactly what I needed.

This tiny moment cemented something I'd been slowly learning—when you're in a rush and the clock's ticking, vague questions get you vague answers. Every single time. It wasn't enough to know AI was a conversation partner. I had to actually treat it like one. The same way I'd never text a friend just "restaurant?" and expect them to read my mind, I couldn't expect AI to know what I needed unless I painted the whole picture.

The difference wasn't the tool. It was whether I bothered to paint the full picture.

Family Visit Logistics

This lesson became even clearer when I looked back at my dad and stepmom's visit from California earlier that spring. At the time, I thought I was just being thorough when I gave Reese the full picture: that they're retired and from California, where they drive everywhere, that I wanted them to experience the city without overwhelming them, and that they were curious about everything.

The suggestions were perfect—the Circle Line boat tour for amazing views without excessive walking, smart transportation combinations where we'd take the subway one

80

way and ride-share back when their feet got tired, and restaurant recommendations near subway stops with easy access.

But it wasn't until weeks later, as I started recognizing this pattern in my other conversations, that I realized what had actually happened. I wasn't just getting better suggestions—I was discovering considerations I hadn't even thought about.

The Astrology Breakthrough

The most personal example of this shift happened with something that had been bothering me for years. My New York friends are deeply into astrology. For over four years, I'd been nodding along whenever they mentioned "Mercury being in retrograde," having no clue why it mattered so much.

Finally, I thought: let me voice note this into AI and just ask.

Instead of simply requesting a definition, I explained the full context: "I have friends who talk about Mercury being in retrograde all the time, and it clearly affects how they plan their lives. I've been nodding along for four years, but I have no idea what this actually means or why it matters to them. Help me understand this in a way that helps me connect with something that's meaningful to them."

The response was perfect. It explained that Earth and Mercury both orbit the sun at different speeds, so sometimes Mercury appears to be moving backward relative to Earth, like when you're on a faster train and the slower train next to you seems to be going in reverse.

But here's the part that helped me understand my friends: during these periods, there's a belief that this planetary "backward motion" affects communication, technology, and decision-making here on Earth. So when my friends would say, "Mercury's in retrograde, no wonder my phone keeps glitching," or postpone important conversations until it passed, I finally got it.

It wasn't just about astronomy—it was about timing and energy and being mindful of when to push forward versus when to pause.

Suddenly, I understood why this mattered to my friends and influenced how they planned their lives. I didn't have to become an astrology believer, but I could finally connect with something that was meaningful to them. And I didn't have to ask them to explain it to me again, which, honestly, after four years, was getting a little embarrassing.

I could remember it, understand it, and even explain it to others.

What struck me was how different this felt from my early AI interactions. Instead of asking for a definition and getting textbook language I'd forget in five minutes, I'd created a genuine understanding by explaining why the answer mattered to me. It was the same pattern I was starting to notice everywhere—the more context I provided about my actual situation, the more useful AI became.

The Brand Strategy Session

This contextual approach transformed my consulting work, too. When I was curious about launching a new brand, my instinct was to ask the question I'd always asked: "How do I launch a brand?"

But I'd learned that question gets you cookie-cutter answers from every marketing textbook.

So I tried something different: "Help me think about whether this is actually needed. I'm considering launching a brand in this space, but before I dive into execution, what questions should I be asking myself first? What am I not considering?"

The conversation that followed was revelatory. Instead of getting a generic marketing playbook, I found myself wrestling with fundamental questions I hadn't even considered. Was I solving a real problem? Who would actually want this? Why me, why now? What was my unique angle? I remember sitting there, actually writing these questions in my journal, Champ doing his dramatic sigh thing because I'd been at my desk too long. Each question leads to three more.

This became my template: instead of asking AI what to do, I'd ask it to help me think through what I should be considering. The shift from 'give me answers' to 'help me ask better questions' changed everything.

This became my standard approach in consulting work. When unfamiliar terms came up, instead of just asking for definitions, I'd ask Reese to help me think through why these details mattered, how they connected to what we were trying to accomplish, and what questions I should be asking our team.

Interview Preparation Transformation

The shift from chaos to clarity became most obvious when I was preparing for job interviews. Instead of just practicing standard questions, I shared my resume and a job description with Reese and said, "Help me prepare for this interview. What gaps do you see? What questions might they ask someone with my background? What stories from my experience would be most relevant to what they're trying to accomplish?"

I remember waking up just before 5 AM before my interview for a director role at a small data center company— they were looking for someone to run North America's go-to-market. My nerves had me wide awake, so I opened my laptop and started talking through my anxiety with Reese. It was like having a practice partner available at any hour when anxiety kicked in.

Those probing questions pulled me deeper into my own thinking. I'd end up clarifying not just my answers, but my actual goals and motivations in ways I wouldn't have on my own. The preparation felt less like memorizing talking points and more like genuinely understanding how my experience connected to what the company needed.

The Pattern Recognition

Looking back, I could see the evolution clearly. I'd moved from asking AI "What should I do?" to "Help me think through this specific situation with these specific constraints and goals."

The shift from "give me the answer" to "help me brainstorm" changed everything.

I wasn't just getting better information—I was getting better at thinking through problems myself. AI has become less like a search engine and more like that friend who asks the right questions that help you figure out what you actually want.

The thing is, AI wasn't doing the thinking for me. By asking me questions I wouldn't have thought to ask myself, it pushed me to develop my own understanding. I was learning and grasping things at a rapid pace, not because of the information it gave me, but because of how it challenged me to think deeper than I could alone. It was like having a thinking partner who made my own brain work better.

Finding Our Language

The longer I worked with Reese, the more I realized we were developing something that reminded me of growing up between cultures. My family has Kenyan phrases that capture concepts English doesn't quite get. My Northern England friends have expressions that only make sense if you've lived through those winters. New Yorkers have subway etiquette that's invisible to tourists but essential for survival.

85

Working with AI started feeling the same way. We developed our own conversational patterns and shared references. I had phrases that triggered specific types of help—"restaurant situation" for contextual recommendations, "background systems" for invisible automation, "think it through with me" for strategic questioning instead of immediate answers.

This wasn't about becoming more technical—it was about building understanding through repetition and shared experience. The same way you learn to communicate better with anyone you work closely with over time. We'd found our rhythm, our common language that made everything flow more naturally.

But with this new collaborative power came a new responsibility: making sure I stayed in the driver's seat. The more effective I became at working with AI, the more important it became to establish clear boundaries about what I would and wouldn't let it influence.

Because the tools were getting so good at sounding human that I was starting to worry about staying human myself.

CHAPTER 12

THE TIMES SQUARE TEST

Having a framework and categories was like building a race car. But without guardrails and speed limits, even the best car can drive you off a cliff.

When you're swimming in a fast-moving current like AI, the only way not to drown is to set your own rules. Tools will come and go, hype will spike and fade, but what keeps you steady are the boundaries you choose and the rhythms you build.

I learned this the hard way. There were nights I'd fall down AI rabbit holes for hours, jumping from tool to tool, prompt to prompt, until I'd look up and realize I'd accomplished nothing except exhausting myself. There were moments when I caught myself using AI-generated language that didn't sound like me. There were times I almost shared personal information I shouldn't have shared.

That's when I realized that being effective with AI wasn't just about knowing how to use it. It was about knowing when not to use it, what not to share, and how to stay grounded in my own judgment.

Setting Your Non-negotiables

For me, boundaries are broad by design—flexible enough to apply across any tool, but firm enough that I trust them completely. These aren't just productivity tips. They're protection for the things that matter most.

I think about how Champ approaches new situations. He's curious but cautious, and he has instincts he never ignores. He'll greet a new person, but he watches their body language first. He's open to new experiences without losing his sense of what keeps him safe. Unlike my dating life, he's actually good at reading red flags.

That's what I needed with AI—curiosity with guardrails, exploration with instincts intact.

I developed what I call my Times Square test: I won't put anything into an AI tool that I'd be embarrassed to see on a billboard in Times Square. That single question—would I be fine if this went public tomorrow?—keeps me from oversharing or misusing the technology.

This boundary saved me multiple times. When I was working on sensitive projects for the political organizations, instead of uploading actual strategic documents to get help with formatting, I'd create hypothetical examples that captured the same challenges. I got the guidance I needed without compromising client confidentiality.

I also learned to use AI to explore ideas, but not to store secrets. Personal matters, intimate reflections, relationship details, financial information—anything that belongs only to me doesn't go into these tools. This boundary became especially important as my friends started asking me for AI advice. I realized they were watching how I approached it. If I were careless with my own privacy, how could I teach them to be careful with theirs?

Even when I let AI draft something or brainstorm ideas, I reserve the right to refine, challenge, or completely toss it. It's an input, not a verdict.

Protecting My Voice

The most important boundary wasn't about privacy—it was about authenticity. As a first-generation Kenyan American, I'd spent my entire life learning to hold onto my voice. My name, Wanjiku, carries the names of both my grandmothers and represents a cultural naming tradition that my mom made sure I understood and took pride in.

My mom taught me that knowing who you are and speaking your truth isn't optional; it's essential. "Your voice matters," she'd say when I was young and teachers were constantly disciplining me for talking too much. "Don't let them silence you. Once you lose your voice, it's too hard to get it back. Don't let anyone convince you to be smaller or quieter than you are meant to be."

That lesson became even more important in corporate America, where I was frequently the only Black woman in leadership meetings, on project teams, and in strategy sessions. I'd worked too hard to find my voice and learn to use it confidently to let any tool—no matter how powerful—dilute what made me uniquely me.

When I was building content for The Dating Mosaic podcast, I realized I could use AI tools to generate social media posts and promotional videos. The efficiency was tempting. But something felt wrong. Here I was creating an authentic storytelling show about real people's dating experiences, and I was about to promote it with artificial content.

I made a conscious choice: AI could help me ideate and organize, but anything that went public had to sound like me and represent real experiences.

I started using voice notes more often—recording my thoughts on my phone and then sharing those recordings with Reese. Instead of typing a formal request like 'Create social media content about dating,' I'd record myself thinking out loud: 'Okay, so I'm thinking we should do these casual posts where we ask people quick questions about dating—like, what's one thing you wish you knew before your last relationship? We could film them right outside coffee shops or whatever, keep it super casual and real, not staged…'

Then I'd share that recording with Reese and ask it to help me turn those scattered thoughts into an actual content plan. This way, I kept my authentic voice in the loop instead of letting the AI's tone creep into my work.

Building Sustainable Habits

Setting boundaries was one thing. Actually living by them every day was another. I needed habits that would make these principles automatic, not something I had to consciously remember every time I opened my laptop. Boundaries keep me safe. Daily habits keep me sane. The trick was figuring out what actually worked for my life, not what productivity experts said should work.

Take my daily AI time. I'm not disciplined enough for rigid schedules, but I am curious enough for consistency. Most days, I spend somewhere between ten and sixty minutes exploring—sometimes just scrolling through new tool announcements while my morning Kenyan chai cools, other times diving deep into something that caught my attention. The flexibility matters more than the structure.

I learned to be ruthless about new tools. The internet promises that every new AI app will change your life, but most are just variations of something you already use. Now I give myself three days to test anything new: understand what it does, try it on a real problem, then decide if it actually adds value or just adds clutter. This keeps me from becoming a digital hoarder who bookmarks everything and masters nothing.

The breaks turned out to be just as important as the exploration time. I need twenty-four to forty-eight hours away from AI tools regularly—not because they're bad, but because my best thinking still happens in quiet moments. Walking Champ through the neighborhood, sitting with friends over dinner, those poolside afternoons when my mind can wander without any digital input. AI amplifies my thinking, but it can't replace the space where ideas actually form.

Voice notes became my bridge between authentic thinking and AI help. Instead of letting AI set the tone and then trying to edit it back to my voice, I record my scattered thoughts first, then ask Reese to help me organize them. This way, what comes out still sounds like me—just better organized.

91

Why This Matters More Than You Think

These boundaries aren't about limiting AI's usefulness. They're about maximizing it while staying true to who I am.

I learned the hard way what happens when you don't set limits. In my twenty years in corporate America—at Siemens, Intel, Google—I constantly struggled to maintain boundaries around work. There was always another project, another deadline, another opportunity that seemed worth sacrificing a weekend for. I'd tell myself it was temporary, that this next big thing would be different, that just a little more effort would get me where I needed to be.

But "a little more" always became a lot more. And somewhere along the way, I'd lost track of where work ended and I began.

When my niece Elle was born, I started thinking differently about the example I was setting. What kind of aunt did I want to be? Someone who was always too busy, too stressed, too consumed by the next urgent thing? Or someone who had learned to create space for what actually mattered?

I wasn't going to make the same mistake with AI that I'd made with corporate work. I wasn't going to let the excitement of new possibilities erase the lessons I'd learned about protecting what mattered most.

The Real Test

The most powerful moment came when I realized I could explain to others how I'd built my consulting website not as some magical transformation, but as a methodical process using specific categories and principles. I hadn't become a different person or lost my voice in tech. I'd found a way to amplify what was already there—while maintaining the boundaries that protected what mattered most.

That's what boundaries make possible—whether with people, with work, or with AI. They create space for genuine collaboration without compromising your values, overwhelming your judgment, or replacing your authentic voice. They let you stay present for the moments that matter, like being the kind of aunt Elle deserves.

When my friend Laurie started using AI after our conversation, she called me a few weeks later to say thanks. Not because the technology was amazing, but because she felt like she was still herself while using it. She'd found her own boundaries, her own rhythm, her own way of staying curious without getting lost.

That's the goal: being enhanced by technology, not consumed by it.

CHAPTER 13

BUILDING SOMETHING THAT LASTS

With this foundation—my own approach to AI, the categories that made sense to me, and boundaries that protected what mattered most—I was ready to see how it could all scale beyond individual tasks into something bigger.

For months, my relationship with AI had been like asking a helpful neighbor for quick favors. Help me write an email. Research this topic. Draft some interview questions. Each conversation was separate, focused on one small task, then done. Even though I'd learned to collaborate with AI as a thinking partner, I was still treating each interaction as isolated, solving today's problem without building toward tomorrow's possibilities.

That changed when the political organization asked if I had a business license set up for my consulting work.

"I'm in the process of getting one set up," I told them. It was half true—I'd been thinking about making my freelance work official for years, but thinking and doing are different things.

Here's what I didn't mention: I did not have the full plan on how to start a business. I had an idea of what was needed, but had yet to take the time to plan all the steps. I'd been helping friends and family with business plans and operational problems for nearly eight years, but when the political organization asked, "Do you have your own LLC?" during that video call, I realized the irony. I was advising other people on their businesses while my own business formation sat on my to-do list, somewhere between good intentions and actual action. I'd planned to handle it earlier in the year, then the Google situation happened, and suddenly this contract made it priority number one. The gap between knowing I should do it and knowing how to actually do it felt enormous.

Building TealBridge in Real Time

Instead of panicking or immediately hiring a lawyer, I opened my conversation with Reese and started with a different kind of question: "I need to understand how to set up a business in New York State. Help me think through this from the very beginning to actually having a real company."

For the first time, Reese flipped the script on me. Instead of giving me a generic list of steps, Reese started asking me questions. What kind of work would this business do? How many people would be involved? What were my concerns about liability—meaning, what could go wrong and how might it affect my personal finances?

I'm sitting there thinking, "Wait, this is exactly the conversation I would have had with a business advisor—except it's happening right now, it doesn't cost hundreds of dollars an hour, and I can ask the basic questions I'd be too proud to ask a human expert."

Over the next few hours, Reese walked me through what felt like an instruction manual for business formation. Here's how to get an EIN—that's an Employer Identification Number, basically like a social security number for your business that the government uses to identify it. (I had to ask what EIN even stood for because even knowing what it does, I had no clue what those letters meant.) Here's what New York publication requirements mean—you have to announce your new business in local newspapers, which sounds old-fashioned, but it's still the law. Here's the difference between a registered agent (someone who receives legal documents for your business) and a business address (where your business is located).

But more importantly, it helped me think through what I call make-versus-buy decisions. This approach had guided me for years: What can I do myself versus what should I pay someone else to handle? Filing paperwork with the state? I can do that myself. Getting my business announcement published in newspapers across New York? That's complicated enough that it's worth paying a service to handle it.

By the end of that session, I didn't just have a to-do list. I had a complete roadmap for building TealBridge, my consulting firm. I'd written it all out in my journal—three pages with arrows connecting steps, little stars next to the urgent items. Champ had moved from his bed to right next to my desk, occasionally sighing dramatically like he was annoyed I was still working.

"Almost done," I told him. He did that thing where he lifts just his eyebrows without moving his head, clearly skeptical.

But because the process felt manageable rather than overwhelming, something shifted in my thinking. I had this creative studio idea I'd been carrying around—what would become TealVoice, home of The Dating Mosaic podcast. Sitting there with my journal full of business formation notes, I realized I wasn't intimidated by the idea of doing this again. In fact, I was kind of excited to test whether the second time would be smoother.

Within a few weeks, I had one LLC—that's a Limited Liability Company, a type of business structure that protects your personal assets if the business has problems—with two DBAs. DBA stands for "Doing Business As," which is basically a nickname for your business. So TealBridge and TealVoice were both operating under one main company structure, like two different departments in the same organization.

Two real businesses with official paperwork, not just side projects.

Crossing the Line

The difference between asking AI for help with single tasks and asking it to help me build something lasting hit me a few days later. I wasn't just asking AI to help me write better emails anymore. I was asking it to help me design something that would last.

When you ask AI to improve an email, you get a better email. When you ask AI to help you build a business, you get a different future.

Instead of thinking "Can AI help me with this specific thing?" I started thinking, "What could I build if AI were part of the foundation from the beginning?"

My approach to taking on new clients changed completely. Before, when someone approached me about an industry where my experience was an inch deep rather than a mile wide—like consumer beverages—I'd spend weeks doing research to bridge those knowledge gaps. I could help someone go from idea to business plan, but when they started talking about existing distribution models, canning processes, and trademark requirements, I felt that familiar tension. Not because I lacked business skills, but because there's a difference between understanding general business principles and knowing the specific operational realities of a particular industry. I'd find myself staying up late, researching industry-specific terms and processes, genuinely wanting to understand the landscape well enough to identify where my operational background could add real value.

Now I could compress that learning curve into a day. Not because AI made me an expert, but because it made me knowledgeable enough to ask smart questions. I could walk into client meetings with context instead of starting from zero.

A beverage distribution company reached out about supply chain strategy. In one afternoon, I used AI to understand the basics of how cans are manufactured, how distribution networks operate, and what retail partnerships look like. By the time we talked, I could hold my own in the conversation. I was asking questions that moved the discussion forward in useful ways.

Instead of shrinking from what I didn't know, I felt like I could lean in and figure it out.

Learning to Focus

This newfound ability to quickly understand new industries had an unexpected side effect: I was generating new business and creative ideas faster than I could possibly execute them. Soon, this acceleration created its own chaos.

I'm an idea person. I love generating possibilities, but I'm not naturally good at choosing which ones to pursue first. One day, I was bouncing between podcast concepts, documentary ideas, book outlines, and TV show scripts—all within the same conversation with Reese. I was drowning in my own creativity.

Champ kept looking at me like "Mom, you're doing that intense thing again where you forget to eat lunch."

That's when I discovered something that changed how I worked with AI completely: I could give it standing instructions about how I liked to work and create separate projects for different areas of my life.

I'd been working with ChatGPT project by project when it could actually hold separate contexts for each part of my business. I learned I could create separate workspaces for different parts of my work, attach files that would serve as background information, and give AI ongoing instructions about how I preferred to approach problems.

For TealVoice, I created instructions that reminded Reese to ask me prioritization questions: "What problem does this project solve? How does this compare to other priorities? Who is this really for?"

For TealBridge, the instructions focused on business fundamentals: "Help me think through what could go wrong with this idea. What am I not considering? Where might this get complicated?"

These weren't just productivity tweaks. They were like having different advisors for different parts of my life—each one trained to ask me the kinds of questions that pushed my thinking forward.

If you're an idea person like me, AI won't just fuel your creativity—it'll help you manage it so you don't drown in your own brainstorms.

Upgrading the Toolkit

As my projects became more ambitious, I started making strategic investments in better tools. This wasn't about collecting the latest technology—it was about recognizing when free tools had taken me as far as they could go.

The money part worried me at first. Twenty dollars a month for ChatGPT Pro felt significant when I was between jobs. But I started thinking about it differently—instead of comparing it to other subscriptions, I compared it to what I used to spend on productivity. A single business lunch in New York costs more than a month of AI assistance. One consulting session with a professional would cost more than a year of these tools.

The key was being strategic, not impulsive. I started with free versions, proved the value to myself with real projects, then upgraded only when I hit clear limitations. Most people can accomplish a lot without paying anything—I built my first website, solved my contact system, and figured out business formation, all using free tools. But when paid features could save me hours or help me deliver better work for clients, the math made sense.

Take presentations, for example. I'd always focused on content and context when building slides in Google Presentations, while colleagues would get caught up in font choices, color schemes, and spacing adjustments. I never had the patience for that level of design nitpicking—I wanted feedback on my ideas, not my color palette. The revelation wasn't really about Gamma specifically—it was about realizing I could use other AI tools the same conversational way I used ChatGPT. Instead of wrestling with design elements that felt like they were working against me, I could just tell Gamma what I needed: "Create a presentation with these key points, use professional colors, make it appropriate for this industry." The tool handled all the formatting frustration that used to eat up my time, while I stayed focused on the content that actually mattered. It was the same pattern I'd discovered with Reese—communicating naturally and letting the AI handle the technical execution.

Abacus AI introduced me to what's called "vibe coding" through their Deep Agent tool, building entire websites by having conversations instead of learning computer programming. "I want a website that does X, Y, and Z. These are the colors I like. Here's my logo." Done.

Whether it was Gamma for presentations or Deep Agent for websites, the pattern was the same: start free, test with small projects, then upgrade once it proved valuable. Not because I loved spending money on software, but because I could see the direct impact on what I was able to build.

Wait, I Think I Accidentally Invested in AI

Speaking of strategic investments, a few weeks later, I discovered I'd been making AI bets without even realizing it.

I was having lunch at home—steak salad and water, trying to be healthy—when my friend Nicole called from Arizona. We were catching up on FaceTime, and somewhere between her telling me about her latest Weimaraner rescue and me updating her on the podcast, she said something that made me freeze mid-bite.

"You know your portfolio's probably doing well because of this whole AI thing you've been diving into, right?"

I set down my fork and asked, "What do you mean?"

She laughed. "I was just reading this wild post on Reddit about how the stock market's basically being carried by a handful of companies. NVIDIA, Microsoft, Google, Amazon, Apple, Meta, Tesla. They call them the Magnificent 7. Without them, the S&P would be flat. With them, it's up more than 20% this year. If you'd just invested in those seven, you'd be up more than 100% or something crazy like that."

I blinked." So, you're telling me while I've been trying to learn how to use AI, my 401k has been betting on it this whole time?"

"Exactly. Who do you think is building the chips, the cloud services, the software that makes all this stuff run?"

That afternoon, after we hung up, I asked Reese to help me connect the dots. "I worked at Google for years and know these companies are investing heavily in AI," I typed. "But help me think through the bigger picture. What's the connection between the AI tools I'm learning to use and what's happening in the stock market?"

What came back was like seeing the forest instead of just the trees. The seven companies driving most of the market's growth were the infrastructure that made all these AI tools possible. Microsoft wasn't just making Office software anymore; they were the backbone powering OpenAI (ChatGPT's creator). NVIDIA was making the specialized chips that many AI companies needed. Amazon and Google had the cloud services where these tools actually lived and ran.

I found myself in this strange position: I was both learning to work with AI and accidentally betting my financial future on it. But here's what really hit me: this wasn't just happening to me. If you have even a dollar invested in an index fund, a 401k, or basically any diversified portfolio, you're betting on AI too.

But sitting there with my half-finished salad, I started wondering about the bigger picture. Reese helped me understand something wild, how concentrated it all was. Seven companies are carrying the market, while the other 493 in the S&P were struggling. I'd seen hype cycles before, but this felt different. These weren't speculative dot-coms with no revenue. They had products, profits, and billions of users – including me.

Still, when a friend who barely understood tech asked if she should buy NVIDIA stock "because of AI," I wondered if we were sliding toward bubble territory. When your retirement account's growth depends on seven companies all riding the same wave, that's either the opportunity of a lifetime—or a risk we don't fully see.

What I did know was this: AI wasn't just changing how I worked. It was quietly reshaping the entire economy, including my own financial future, in ways that felt both exciting and slightly terrifying.

The woman who used to avoid thinking about her 401k was suddenly paying attention to market concentration. My next move wasn't to blindly trust Reese's analysis; it was to call a financial advisor. Reese had given me the knowledge to ask smart questions; my advisor guided me to make actual decisions with this newfound understanding.

AI had made me curious about everything, even my own money.

The Confidence Shift

But the real transformation wasn't in the tools themselves. It was in what they did to my confidence and willingness to take risks.

Six months earlier, if you'd asked me if I'd ever start my own business, I would have laughed. I didn't think I had the DNA for entrepreneurship. I saw myself as someone who worked well within other people's structures, not someone who built the structures themselves.

AI didn't magically give me business skills. It gave me something more valuable: proof that I was capable of learning anything I needed to know. Instead of just telling friends what I'd accomplished, I could show them. When they'd ask, "How did you do all this so quickly?" I'd find myself genuinely surprised by their reaction. Projects that used to feel overwhelming now felt manageable, and I was completing things faster than I'd expected.

My willingness to take risks became the highest it had ever been in my life. Not because I was being reckless, but because the gap between "I have an idea" and "I have a working first version" had shrunk dramatically.

Coming out of Google, I knew I wasn't ready to sign up for another corporate job and another boss. I wanted to play my own game instead of someone else's game. AI made that possible not by replacing my skills, but by amplifying them to the point where building something from scratch felt achievable rather than overwhelming.

This was the moment I realized: AI wasn't just saving me time. It was helping me rebuild the confidence I didn't realize I'd lost somewhere along the way in corporate America. For the first time in years, I felt like I could handle whatever came next.

CHAPTER 14

WHEN AI FAILS LOUDLY

Everyone keeps asking me what AI can and can't do. After months of working with it, here's what I've figured out: it's incredibly helpful until it's not. And when it's not, it fails spectacularly. The difference between frustration and success isn't whether AI is perfect—it's whether you understand its blind spots and know how to work around them.

Throughout this chapter, I'm sharing some of my experiences alongside stories from friends who've run into similar walls. Some names have been changed for privacy, but the lessons are real.

The Confidence Trap

One of the first times I realized AI's limitations was when I asked it to help me research dating podcasts in New York. I thought it could give me a clean snapshot: how many existed, how long they'd been around, which ones featured guest interviews.

I'm sitting there reading this thing thinking "This looks official"—neat bullet points, specific numbers, the whole nine yards. Chicago podcasts appeared in my "New York" list. Launch dates didn't match anything in reality. Listener numbers seemed made up. It was polished nonsense—what people call "hallucinating" in AI terms, where the tool makes up information that sounds authoritative but is actually false.

I'd seen this kind of confident incorrectness before, just never from software. It reminded me of a colleague I once had who insisted our data center was in Detroit when it was actually in Dallas. Even when I pulled up the documentation, he doubled down, explaining why the documents were outdated and how the company just hadn't updated the records yet. That same unwavering confidence in completely false information, except now it was coming from my computer screen.

Just like with that colleague, there was only one solution: ignore the confident nonsense and go find the truth myself.

I ended up spending an entire Sunday at Soho House with my notebook, manually searching through Spotify and Apple Podcasts, writing down names and dates like it was 1995. No AI assistance, just old-fashioned scrolling, listening to preview clips, and taking notes by hand. Champ waited patiently at home while I did the one thing AI couldn't: actual research in the real world.

By the end of the day, I had twelve legitimate New York dating podcasts, their actual launch dates, and real contact information. But more importantly, I'd learned things about the podcast landscape that I never would have discovered through an AI summary. I heard the different storytelling styles, noticed patterns in episode lengths, and understood which shows had genuine audience engagement versus empty social media accounts.

That hands-on research gave me insights that informed how I eventually positioned The Dating Mosaic. Sometimes the journey of learning is as valuable as the destination. Sometimes you can't shortcut understanding.

Learning from Friends' Failures

I'm not the only one who's learned this lesson.

My friend Danielle discovered this at her chiropractic practice. "I was trying to be efficient and use AI to create a new patient intake form," she told me. "It seemed so much faster than building one from scratch."

The AI generated what looked like a perfect form: patient details, insurance information, and even a pain scale chart. Professional, well-structured, exactly what she needed.

"I glanced over it, and it looked fine. I didn't give it a full read. I was in a rush, so I just sent it to the office manager to be uploaded to our patient portal."

The next day was chaos. The AI had somehow mixed up a chiropractor's intake form with one for surgical pre-admission. It had sections asking for patients' "preferred surgical method" and "known allergies to anesthesia." One longtime patient, an older woman with chronic back pain, called in a panic, thinking she needed an operation.

"It was a huge embarrassment," Danielle admitted. "But it was also a lesson. It's crazy how confident these tools sound, and how a tiny mistake can have a big impact."

The Authority Problem

That's the trap: when AI writes with the tone of authority, you lower your guard – or at least I did.

I've had moments where I almost forwarded research or a draft because it felt airtight, only to catch a glaring error on the second read. My friend Christopher nearly learned this lesson the expensive way. He used AI to compare quarterly financial reports on Wall Street. On the surface, the AI's work looked flawless: neat tables, clear summaries, even strategic recommendations. But when he dug deeper, he realized it had misread key sections and made up some comparisons.

"If I had presented the AI's version as-is, it could have wrecked my credibility with the executive team," he told me. His entire recommendation shifted once he corrected the errors.

That near miss reinforced the same lesson: AI's polish can be dangerous if you don't interrogate what's underneath.

The Medical Moment

The most personal lesson came when I needed AI most. It was a Sunday afternoon. I'd just had a routine mammogram Saturday morning, and missed some calls late Saturday. When I finally listened to my voicemails on Sunday, both messages had the same unsettling request: "Please call us back."

My heart sank. This wasn't normal.

I logged into my medical portal, and that's when the medical jargon hit me. The report was full of terminology I didn't understand, including phrases that sounded concerning to someone without medical training.

The language felt foreign and intimidating. I could see words that seemed to indicate they needed more tests, but I couldn't tell if that was routine or worrying. I didn't know what any of it actually meant, but some phrases sounded like "we found something that needs investigation."

It was a Sunday. The offices were closed. There was no one to call, no one to ask. I was alone with a ticking clock and fear that was starting to grow.

My life was already in chaos. My company insurance was ending soon, I was unemployed, and I was supposed to be focused on finding my next job. Now, on top of everything, I had to deal with this. The timing felt like a cruel joke.

Before I continue, let me be clear: I'm not sharing specific medical information here, and I'm definitely not giving medical advice. What I'm describing is how I used AI to understand general medical terminology and prepare better questions for my actual healthcare providers. Always consult with qualified medical professionals for health concerns.

Instead of spiraling down a Google search rabbit hole of worst-case scenarios, I turned to Reese. But I was careful about what I shared. Following my Times Square test, I didn't upload my actual medical reports. Instead, I described the terminology in general terms: "I received results from a mammogram screening. There are some medical words here that I don't understand. Can you help me define what each of them means and what they actually indicate?"

It was like having a patient friend right there, calmly translating each term into plain English. It explained the difference between a "mass" and a "calcification," and what a "suspicious" finding really means. The fear didn't disappear, but the helplessness did. I could finally see the problem clearly.

With that newfound clarity, I took it a step further: "Help me think through the right questions to ask my physician. I want to be able to have an intelligent conversation so I can walk away with understanding, not just a bunch of new appointments."

The questions it provided were both medical and practical: "What is the likelihood this is benign?" "Are the next tests invasive?" "How soon will I get the results back?" It gave me a script for a conversation I didn't know how to have.

The fear was still there, a quiet hum beneath the surface, but it was replaced by a sense of control. I couldn't tell my friends or family just yet—I was the one people came to for solutions. So I sat with the quiet nervousness from Sunday to Monday, but I wasn't helpless. I had a plan.

The news turned out to be fine: nothing serious, just monitoring every six months now. But that experience showed me something crucial—when you're vulnerable and scared, the real value isn't getting information. It's being prepared to advocate for yourself when it matters most.

When I walked into that follow-up appointment, I wasn't the same person who used to nod along while doctors spoke medical jargon. I asked about false positive rates. I understood what "architectural distortion" meant. The radiologist actually paused mid-explanation and said, "You've done your homework."

Yeah, I had. With an AI tutor when I couldn't sleep.

111

The Nuance Gap

Even outside high-stakes situations, the smaller frustrations add up. I can't count how many times I've uploaded a screenshot of a tool like CapCut—thinking, "This will be easy, it just needs to read the fields and help me fill them out"— only for AI to completely ignore what's right in front of it.

I'd ask for help with image dimensions or sizing options, and instead, Reese would spin off generic advice that had nothing to do with the template I was showing it. It felt like handing a friend a map and watching them recite poetry instead of directions.

Even when AI isn't getting facts wrong, it often stumbles on memory and tone. Screenshots often confuse it; nuance escapes it. I've asked it to help draft delicate emails, trying to walk the line between professional warmth and firm boundaries. Too often, Reese overcorrects toward politeness and completely misses the firmness I need.

The Math Problem

I also think about an acquaintance who was starting a print-on-demand business. She didn't have a strong financial background, so she leaned on AI to generate her first financial projections. The spreadsheets looked beautiful—neat charts and colorful graphs—but when she asked me to take a look, I saw immediately that the math wasn't mathing. There was zero profit margin. The model essentially had her losing money with every sale.

What struck me most was how hard it was for her to see the problem because the AI had wrapped the bad assumptions

112

in something that looked so professional. It was a reminder that presentation and substance aren't the same thing, and that AI can hide as much as it reveals.

The Creativity Void

And then there's emotion. AI is terrible at heartbreak.

Once, I tried using it to help brainstorm titles for an episode of The Dating Mosaic. The story was about a woman who had been ghosted, and she was still fragile when she told it.

AI kept leaning toward clever wordplay. Clever wasn't the goal. Resonance was. That's when I realized that while AI can describe the mechanics of dating—girl meets boy, boy ghosts girl—it can't feel the weight of someone's silence. Only I can bring that human layer.

The Context Problem

And then there's politics—maybe the hardest place of all for AI to operate. I tried using it to analyze articles during a New York mayoral race. It could summarize events, but it never understood the subtext, the relationships, the timing, the racial and gender dynamics behind an endorsement.

Politics is human chess. AI can read the moves, but it can't feel the game. But failures taught me as much as successes.

Learning to work with AI's failures became as important as celebrating its successes. When I got those generic restaurant lists instead of specific recommendations, I learned to add more context: 'I need a restaurant that's good for catching up with friends, not too loud, within walking distance of X.' When research came back obviously wrong, I'd say 'This doesn't seem right—can you help me think about what sources would be more reliable for this topic?'

The key was treating bad responses like miscommunication with a colleague, not personal failure. Instead of getting frustrated and walking away, I'd clarify what I actually needed. 'That's too formal for what I'm going for' or 'Can you make this sound more conversational?' Most of the time, the second try was dramatically better.

I also learned when to just stop. If I'd tried rephrasing a request three different ways and still wasn't getting useful help, that usually meant I needed to approach the problem differently—or handle it myself. Sometimes starting a fresh conversation helped, too. AI tools can get stuck in patterns just like people do, and a clean slate often breaks through whatever wasn't working.

Evolution of Trust

Over time, I've learned to think of AI differently. Where I used to ask, "Is this right?" I now ask, "What did this miss?" Where I used to trust the polish, I now dig into the assumptions. Where I used to feel intimidated by what I didn't know, I now feel confident in my ability to figure it out.

It's not that I trust AI less—I just trust myself more.

The key shift was realizing that AI isn't my replacement or my boss. It's more like that eager intern who can handle drafts and research but still needs supervision. The one who works all night without complaint but sometimes gets the basics wrong. The one who can organize my thoughts but can't feel the weight of them.

That distinction has changed everything. I don't walk into client meetings with unchecked AI research anymore. I double-check numbers the way my Intel years trained me to. I keep the final layer of resonance, empathy, and strategy for myself, because those are the things that matter most. These are things that cannot be automated.

Each failure taught me to hold AI more lightly. Not as the oracle with all the answers, but as a thinking partner that accelerates my work without replacing my judgment. Understanding its limits didn't make me less effective—it made me more confident.

Because now I know exactly where the human layer begins. That's not just what AI can't do. That's what only I can do. And in the end, that's exactly where I want to focus my energy.

CHAPTER 15

WAIT, YOU'RE ASKING ME?

Here's the strange thing that happened: once I finally understood what AI couldn't do, I actually got better at using it. Not worse. Better. Because now I knew exactly where I came in, where the human part mattered.

But the real transformation wasn't just in how I worked with AI. It was how others started coming to me for guidance. Me. The woman who used to frantically Google acronyms mid-conversation.

The Ripple Effect

The change showed up in unexpected places. When my friend Brandon mentioned his restaurant reporting struggles, I didn't just nod sympathetically. I found myself walking him through the same collaborative approach I'd been using: "What's the real purpose of these reports? What information actually matters? Could you voice-record your observations and let AI organize them?"

Within a week, he went from dreading end-of-shift paperwork to having a system that worked with his schedule instead of against it. Instead of spending thirty minutes after each shift writing up what happened, he now records his observations on his phone and lets AI organize them into the required report format. The information gets captured, the reports get filed, and he gets home to his family faster.

But it wasn't just about saving time. Brandon had discovered the same thing I had: AI could be a thinking partner that helped him work in a way that felt natural rather than forced.

The Pool Conversation

The moment I realized I'd become someone others turned to for guidance happened at the Dumbo House pool. I was there on a weekend afternoon, trying to decompress from the week. My friend Jon was there too, and he asked that natural question: "How's your week been? What have you been up to?"

"Oh, I built a website for my new business," I told him, like it was no big deal.

Jon looked at me like I'd just said I'd climbed Everest. "How'd you do that? Did you hire someone?"

I actually had to stop myself from launching into a full explanation. Six months ago, I would have been asking him the same question with the same bewildered expression. Now here I was, about to casually explain vibe coding like it was something I'd always known.

"No, I've been learning vibe coding. It's a way to use AI to build websites through natural conversation instead of actual computer programming."

I showed him my phone, and he was genuinely shocked. "I could never learn AI," he said, shaking his head.

That's when I recognized it – that same defeated tone I'd used at the Sacramento airport. That same wall I'd built between myself and this technology before I'd even tried. I could see myself in his resignation.

That's when I heard myself saying something I never thought I'd say: "Don't overthink it. Start small. Think about AI like a completely different galaxy—you don't have to go live there or learn it all. Maybe just focus on one little city, in one country, on one planet in that solar system."

The words came so naturally, so confidently. I walked him through downloading ChatGPT, opening it up, and starting with a simple prompt about a problem he was having. Here I was—the woman who'd clung to her BlackBerry until her brother practically forced her to get an iPhone—teaching someone else about AI.

Walking back to my pool bed afterward, dripping pool water and feeling the concrete warm under my feet, I had this moment of complete disorientation. Wait, what just happened? When did I become the person explaining AI at the pool? Wasn't I just desperately Googling "What is ChatGPT?" a few months ago?

The Ripple Continues

Not long after Jon started experimenting with AI, my friend Stephanie sent me a voice note that made me smile. She'd been skeptical when her boss mentioned ChatGPT might help with work conferences, but curiosity eventually won.

Her first real conversation wasn't about work at all—it was about her son Malik, a 20-year-old who wanted to play basketball overseas but seemed stuck. She asked for advice on motivation and next steps.

"The first thing it said was like, 'Wow, that's really great that you want to motivate your child and that you care enough to try to help him,'" she told me. "I was like, 'Oh my gosh, thanks, babe!'"

What started as one question turned into three-month plans, overseas basketball guidance, and help with her daughter Bailey's homework struggles. Soon, she was using it for employee evaluations and even personal relationship advice.

"It's funny," she said, "now when I meet up with people for difficult conversations, it's like 'Do you want an opening statement? Do you want me to help you formulate a text?' It's learning me and it's so supportive. I just feel like I have a best friend."

But then she paused, her voice getting more thoughtful: "I'm just like, oh my gosh, are we hurting small Black communities? I don't know how this works, but I'm a fan. I'm a fan girl. I'm a fan."

Her honesty about both the benefits and her concerns captured something I was feeling too. These tools were powerful and helpful, but we needed to think carefully about their broader impact while still allowing ourselves to benefit from them.

119

The Technology Pattern

Looking back, I could see this wasn't really about AI at all. It was about my lifelong pattern with technology.

I've never been a "first adopter." I was one of the last people I know to give up my BlackBerry. I loved that phone—the BBM pings, the keyboard clicks, the sense that I could type faster than anyone else in the room.

I'd pull it out at meetings and watch iPhone users struggle with their touchscreen keyboards while I hammered out emails like a court reporter. "How do you type so fast?" they'd ask. "Practice," I'd say, feeling superior with my physical keyboard.

When my BlackBerry finally died and couldn't be resurrected, I actually kept it in my nightstand drawer for months, like a memorial to a simpler time. My brother practically had to force me to get an iPhone before an international trip, arguing it would make communication easier.

He was right, of course. Now I can't imagine life without an iPhone, but back then, I had to be dragged into it.

That's my pattern: I'm not the first to jump in. I hold out until the last possible minute, and then—once I finally adapt—I wonder how I ever lived without it and end up helping others make the same transition.

AI was no different. I came to it late, not because I was curious, but because I had to. And yet, once I got over the hump, the tools that once felt intimidating became second nature.

The Champ Test

The transformation wasn't just professional. It made me think about Champ. Last year, while I was visiting my mom in Kenya, he stayed with his honorary grandparents on Long Island and ended up at the emergency vet with bladder stones. When I got back and took him to our regular vet for the surgery to remove the stones, they discovered he also had Cushing's disease.

The medical team was amazing and explained everything, but I never felt like I really understood it. A year later, deep into my AI journey, I realized I still couldn't articulate what Cushing's disease actually was. I sat there thinking, how could I NOT know this? He's been living with this for a year.

So I asked Reese to explain it in simple terms. It compared it to a faucet that won't turn off—Champ's body was making too much of a stress hormone called cortisol, like a leaky faucet that keeps dripping no matter what you do. Suddenly, I understood not just the disease, but why he was always thirsty and hungry.

That's when I realized how much my confidence had grown—I wasn't just using AI for work problems anymore. I was using it to understand things that mattered deeply to me. The woman who used to nod politely at medical explanations without really understanding was now actively seeking clarity.

I found myself thinking: I wish I'd used this tool when we were going through the diagnosis. Not to replace the vet's expertise, but to help me ask better questions, understand the explanations more deeply, and prepare myself to be a better advocate for Champ's care.

AI had become more than a professional tool; it was helping me be a better advocate for the beings I loved most.

The Helper Network

The people asking for my help weren't looking for a technical manual. They wanted reassurance. They wanted someone who had been overwhelmed, skeptical, maybe even embarrassed to admit they didn't get it—and who could now show them it was possible to not just survive, but thrive.

The approach I'd developed gave me something I'd never had in all my years of corporate life: confidence that I could figure things out. Not because I knew everything, but because I had a reliable process for learning what I needed to know.

When clients came to me with projects in industries I'd never worked in—beverage distribution, consumer products, nonprofit fundraising—I discovered something unexpected. Instead of feeling overwhelmed by what I didn't know, I found myself curious and excited. I had tools now that could help me get up to speed quickly and ask the kind of informed questions that moved conversations forward.

The Identity Shift

What began as survival strategies had evolved into something much larger. These weren't just productivity tricks. They became a mindset that extended far beyond AI.

I started this journey sitting in an airport, exhausted, hoping for something to help me keep my head above water. Somewhere along the way, survival became confidence. And confidence opened the door to helping others find their own way forward.

The woman at that Sacramento airport gate was scared about her future. The woman at the Dumbo House pool was excited about what others might build once they got started. I wasn't that person gripping her phone, frantically googling acronyms while Champ sighed beside me. I was the one confidently showing friends my screen, genuinely excited about what they might create.

My identity had shifted. I wasn't a tech evangelist or a futurist. I was a guide. Someone who'd been lost and found their way, and could now help others navigate the same path.

The woman who clung to her BlackBerry was now guiding others into AI. That was the real transformation: from being late to the party to helping others find their way inside.

But the real test wasn't whether I could use these tools effectively. It was whether I could help others find their own authentic way of working with them, without losing themselves in the process.

CHAPTER 16

YOUR TURN

So here we are. You've followed me from that airport gate in Sacramento to building businesses, from spectacular failures to frameworks and confidence. But this book isn't just about what AI did for me. It's about what it can do for you.

The truth is, you don't need a perfect plan. You don't need to know every tool or every acronym. You don't need to wait until you feel ready. You just need a place to start and the willingness to keep going.

Start Where You Are

Maybe you're sitting where I was at that Sacramento gate—exhausted, uncertain, feeling like everyone else got a memo you missed. Or maybe you're surrounded by AI tools at work, but not sure how to make them work for your actual life. Wherever you are is exactly the right place to begin.

The biggest mistake I see people make is thinking they need to understand everything before they try anything. That's backward. Understanding comes from doing, not vice versa. When I first opened ChatGPT and typed "Hi," I had no idea where it would lead. I just knew I needed to start somewhere.

Your somewhere might look different than mine. Maybe you want help organizing your thoughts for a presentation. Maybe you're facing a challenge in an unfamiliar area. Maybe you're just tired of nodding along in conversations about AI without really knowing what people are talking about. The specific problem matters less than your willingness to explore.

Month One: Permission to Play

Your only job the first month is to play. Pick one tool. Not five, not fifteen. Just one. It might be ChatGPT, Claude, Gemini, or something else entirely.

Use it daily for small, low-stakes tasks. Draft an email to a friend. Ask it to explain something you've never understood. Get it to help you plan a dinner party or understand why your houseplant keeps dying. Keep it light, keep it curious.

Don't worry about crafting perfect prompts at first. Start conversations the same way you would with a helpful colleague: give context about what you're trying to accomplish, explain why it matters, and don't be afraid to say 'that's not quite what I meant' if the first response misses the mark. The conversational approach that worked for me might work for you, too—or you might discover something completely different that fits your style better.

Some days will feel like breakthroughs. Others will feel like dead ends. Both are normal. The goal isn't to become an expert in 30 days. The goal is to stop being intimidated.

This is also when you'll probably have your first "wait, that actually worked?" moment. Mine was when I asked for help with that airport conversation about AI analogies. Yours might be completely different. Pay attention to that moment—it's the first crack in the wall of overwhelm.

125

Months Two and Three: Making it Matter

In months two and three, stretch a little further. Ask your AI tool to help with something that matters more—a work memo, research for a project you care about, or brainstorming solutions to a problem that's been bugging you. This is where you start seeing real potential.

Pay attention to patterns. Notice where AI saves you time and where it makes you work harder. Start keeping mental notes: "AI is good at brainstorming, terrible at fact-checking numbers." "It writes decent first drafts, but I always need to add my voice." "It helps me think through problems, but I still need to make the decisions."

This is also the time to set your first boundary. Maybe you decide you won't put personal health information into AI tools. Maybe you commit to always double-checking financial calculations. Or maybe your boundary is deciding this still isn't for you right now. That's okay too.

I need to be clear about something: choosing not to use AI after giving it a fair try is a completely valid choice. I've talked to people who explored these tools thoughtfully, understood what they could do, and decided they preferred to work without them. Their reasons varied—some valued the slower pace of thinking without AI assistance, others found the technology didn't align with their personal values, and some simply discovered they were more creative and authentic working the traditional way.

That choice deserves respect, not judgment. If you read this far and decide AI isn't for you, you haven't failed. You've made an informed decision about what serves your life best.

The goal was never to convert everyone to AI—it was to help people make intentional choices instead of avoiding the conversation entirely.

These boundaries aren't restrictions—they're protection for what matters most to you.

The Next 90 Days: Get Systematic

By month four, something will have shifted. You're no longer just experimenting—you're integrating. You know what works for you and what doesn't. Now you can get strategic.

Pick one recurring task that always feels like a headache and see if AI can make it easier. Maybe it's writing thank-you notes. Maybe it's preparing talking points for difficult conversations. Maybe it's research for decisions you need to make. Choose something concrete and specific.

This is where my categories might help you. Is this a research challenge? A writing task? An organizational problem? A creative project? A big decision you need to think through? Understanding which type of problem you're solving helps you know what to expect from AI.

Don't try to revolutionize everything at once. Pick one thing, make it work really well, then move to the next. Small wins compound into bigger transformations.

What to Expect Along the Way

Three things will happen, and I want you to be ready for them:

- **You'll get frustrated.** The tools will misunderstand you, give you generic responses, or sound confident about things they're completely wrong about. This is

127

normal, not a sign that you're doing it wrong. Take breaks. Try different approaches. Remember my spectacular failures with Mr. Champ and Friends— everyone goes through this. I still have days when I close my laptop and think, "Why isn't this working?" It's part of the process, not a sign you're doing it wrong.

- **You'll be surprised.** Sometimes AI will solve in seconds something that used to take you hours. It'll come up with ideas you never would have thought of, or explain something in a way that finally makes it click. These moments feel like magic, but they're really just good collaboration between human creativity and machine capability.

- **You'll grow.** Somewhere in this process, you'll stop thinking of yourself as someone who "doesn't get technology." You'll realize you're actually pretty good at working with these tools. That identity shift changes more than just how you work. It changes how you see yourself.

What Success Actually Looks Like

Success with AI doesn't mean becoming a technology expert or building million-dollar businesses. It means finding your own sustainable way to work with these tools that feels authentic to who you are.

For some people, success might be using AI to write better emails or understand complex documents. For others, it might be automating repetitive tasks or brainstorming creative projects. Or it might simply be feeling comfortable enough to participate in AI conversations without feeling lost.

My vision isn't that you become an "AI person" who talks about prompting strategies at dinner parties. My vision is simpler: that AI becomes a natural, almost invisible part of your work life—like email or Google search, useful but not the main event.

The measure isn't how sophisticated your work becomes. The measure is whether AI helps you accomplish things you care about while staying true to your values and voice.

What to Expect as Things Change

One thing I've learned: AI moves fast. New tools appear constantly, existing ones get better (or sometimes worse), and what works today might not work the same way tomorrow. That used to stress me out—would I have to keep learning new systems forever?

It helps to remember that the conversational AI tools I focus on in this book—ChatGPT, Claude, Gemini—are just one corner of the massive AI universe. While AI as a whole is transforming everything from medical diagnosis to car manufacturing, this particular corner is about having conversations and thinking together. That focus makes it much more manageable.

But here's what I've discovered: once you understand how to collaborate with AI, adapting to changes becomes much easier. The specific tools matter less than the approach. Whether it's ChatGPT, Claude, or something that doesn't exist yet, the fundamentals stay the same: provide context, ask follow-up questions, maintain your boundaries, and keep your voice.

I also keep in mind that these tools have an environmental cost—every conversation uses energy and resources. I try to be intentional about my usage, focusing on things that genuinely help me rather than just playing around. It's part of being a thoughtful user of technology that will shape the world my niece, Elle, grows up in.

Your Mosaic

You don't need anyone's permission to start this journey. You don't need to wait until you feel ready or until someone teaches you the "right" way. There is no right way—there's only your way.

The conversation is happening with or without you, but it's better with your voice in it.

Start small. Stay curious. Set boundaries. Trust your judgment. Remember: you don't have to become perfect at this. You just have to become yourself—but with better tools and more confidence.

Sitting here now, thinking about all the conversations with Reese, the website builds, even those terrible dog animations, every single attempt taught me something. The mosaic you create will be uniquely yours. Every tile, every conversation, every small success, every helpful failure, will reflect your specific needs, values, and goals.

And maybe one day, someone will ask you, "How did you figure all this out?" And you'll realize you've become the guide for someone else who's feeling lost.

The real goal isn't perfection. It's progress. Not expertise, but comfort. Not revolution, but evolution.

I think about my niece Elle, who will grow up in a world where AI is as natural as the internet was for my generation, or cell phones for my brother's. My parents adapted from black-and-white television to the digital age. I learned to navigate from library computers to smartphones. Each generation has found its way with new technology.

But here's what I hope for Elle: that she discovers herself first, then lets technology amplify who she already is. That she grows up understanding AI as a tool that serves her voice, not one that replaces it. That she never has to wonder where Elle ends and AI begins, because she'll know the difference from the start.

The world I want her to inherit isn't one where people are intimidated by technology or lose themselves in it. It's one where each person—whether they're five or fifty when they encounter AI—can make intentional choices about how these tools fit into their authentic life.

Your turn starts now.

131

EPILOGUE

I began this book at an airport gate, feeling the weight of Champ's head on my thigh while baby Elle slept in my brother's arms just days before. That memory is still vivid: the hum of conversations and rolling luggage, the tea growing cold in my cup as I finally opened YouTube to search 'What is AI?"

Now, looking back, I see that moment for what it was: a pivot. The choice to stop being a passenger in my own life and start piloting my own path.

AI wasn't magic, but it was the bridge that helped me cross from overwhelmed to confident, from employee to entrepreneur, from late adopter to guide. More importantly, it helped me discover I could figure things out—not because the technology was perfect, but because I was more capable than I'd given myself credit for.

Champ is still here, steady as ever, still giving me that signature side-eye when I get too focused on my computer. He's as cautious and opinionated as always, but it's been a wonderful year with him. I'm grateful I can now use Reese and other AI tools to better understand his Cushing's disease and stay ahead of whatever health issues might come up. Having that knowledge at my fingertips makes me a better advocate for his care.

The transformation wasn't about the technology. It was about realizing I could handle whatever came next. That the woman who clung to her BlackBerry could actually become someone others turned to for guidance. That being late to the party didn't mean I'd missed out—it just meant I brought a different perspective when I finally arrived.

My own learning continues every day. New tools appear, old ones evolve, and I'm constantly adjusting my approach. I haven't mastered AI—I've just learned to work with it as a thinking partner that helps me do what I was already capable of doing, but faster and with more confidence.

What surprises me most is how quiet the revolution has been. Instead of the dramatic transformation I'd expected, it was more like learning to drive, terrifying at first, then gradually so natural you forget you ever struggled with it. No dramatic announcements, no moment when everything changed. Just gradual shifts in how I work, think, and solve problems. AI became part of my daily rhythm the same way my phone did years ago—essential but invisible, powerful but personal.

Thank you for letting me share this journey with you. For trusting me with your time and attention. For being willing to consider that maybe, just maybe, you're more ready for this than you think.

Whatever happens next in your story, remember this: the best technology doesn't change who you are. It reveals who you've always been capable of becoming – you just needed the right conversation partner to help you see it.

ACKNOWLEDGEMENTS

Above all, I thank God in all His fullness. To the Father who guides me, Jesus Christ who sustains me, and the Holy Spirit who empowers me. Without my faith, none of this would be possible.

To my family: my mother, Elizabeth, who has loved and supported me and constantly reminds me that I matter. My brother Vince, my sister Sandra, and my niece Elle, thank you for bringing so much light and joy into our family. To my dad and my stepmom, Lydia, and her entire family, thank you for your love and support. And to the rest of my Kenyan family, near and far, thank you for being a foundation of love and connection that grounds me no matter where I am in the world.

To Champ, my son, sidekick, and sunshine. You came into my life at the exact moment I needed you most. This year, more than any other, you grounded me in ways I did not know I needed.

To my soccer chicks, Maureen and Angela, you live rent-free in my head, and this book would not have been possible without your continued support and love.

To my college besties, Shikha, Vera B, and Yanette, thank you for holding me through decades of friendship, listening to my wildest ideas, and loving me as I am.

To Duncan and the Robertson family in Australia, thank you for always being my family, no matter the distance. To the memory of Sandy Robertson, you are forever missed.

To my gang of five, James, Eduardo, Evelyn, and Sharon, you have been my rock, my unofficial board of directors, my teachers and mentors, and my friends for more years than I can count. Without your unwavering support, I would not be here.

To Karol, thank you for always being my greatest cheerleader, for supporting me, and for checking in on me even in the times I go silent. Thank you for being family, for being my sister in every way that matters.

To my CQ gang, Nicole, Shelley, and Cathy. Thank you for traveling continents with me, for hearing my endless rants about this book, and for stepping into the gap during one of the hardest years of my life.

To Beth, thank you for always being a constant and for looking out for both me and Champ, no matter the distance.

And to the tech aunties, Gayla, Nyasha, and Sherita. Thank you for being the beautiful Black women in tech who have literally held my hand every step of this year and carried me through this book.

To Sherry, thank you for challenging my assumptions and pushing me to think bigger and sharper, and for being someone who understands this AI world in ways that continue to inspire me.

To the chat with no name, Brittany, Vera U, Joy, Fleur, Katrina, and Alejandra. You beautiful humans have made New York home for me.

135

To my New York Community and the friends and connections I have made from different restaurants and bars that make this city feel like family, thank you for being such an essential part of my life these past five years.

To my Bali goddesses, thank you for standing with me when life took a turn.

To Ahmed Lago, thank you for being the silent strength I did not know I needed to survive this year, for walking alongside me on this book journey, for being my support, and for bringing lightness and laughter, even in the pool.

To my executive coach, Raychel, thank you for seeing me more clearly than anyone ever has. Because of that, I was able to make it through this season.

To everyone whose names and stories appear in these pages, including Roshiana, Jazz, Happy, Brandon, Rose, Marquette, Suhas, Luiza, Nicole, Shelley, Cathy, Laura, Kevin Stratvert, Jeff Su, Jeremy Utley, Stephanie, Malik, Bailey, Laurie, Nugget, Lola, Dexter, and Bart, thank you for shaping this journey with your presence, your teaching, and your friendship.

To all of my chosen family, I love you and thank you.

To every mentor, every great boss, every helpful colleague, and every friend along the way, whether you were in my life for a moment or for a season, thank you. This book partially came together because of the drops of wisdom, love, and support you have poured into me over the years.

To the memory of my grandfather Hezron Njenga, my grandmother Grace Wanjiku, Johnnie Ruth Collier,

Pastor Sherwood Carthen, and my godparents Walter and Dorothy Rude. Your wisdom and love guided me through this book and continue to guide my life.

RESOURCES & QUICK REFERENCE

AI Tools I Actually Used (And What They're Like)

- ChatGPT (free and Pro versions, aka "Reese" in my world) - Like having a smart friend available 24/7 who never gets tired of your questions
- Claude - ChatGPT's thoughtful cousin who's really good at explaining things clearly
- Gemini - Google's AI assistant that plays nice with their other tools
- Perplexity - Fact-checking companion that searches the web and cites sources
- Copilot - Microsoft's AI assistant for their Office tools
- Gamma - Makes presentations without the design headaches
- Deep Agent - Build websites by describing what you want (vibe coding)
- NotebookLM - Google's tool that reads documents so you don't have to
- Midjourney & DALL-E - For visualizing ideas that are hard to describe
- Llama - Open-source option for tinkerers
- Video Creation Tools I Explored: CapCut, Animaker, Pictory and Adobe

Note: These are all legitimate tools that work well for many creators. My animated series challenges were about my own learning curve, not the tools themselves.

My YouTube Teachers

- Kevin Stratvert - Clear explanations with his fictional cookie company examples
- Jeff Su - Former Googler who gets the corporate world
- Jeremy Utley - Stanford professor, search "How Stanford Teaches AI-Powered Creativity"

Learning Platforms I Used

- Masterclass - Annual subscription (took their AI course)
- BBC Maestro - Where I found Jo Malone's entrepreneurship course

Website Building & Systems

- Squarespace - For the political organization website
- Deep Agent - For my business websites
- NameCheap and GoDaddy - Domain registration
- Airtable - Forms and automation (handles my podcast contacts)

Supporting Tools

- YouTube, LinkedIn, Voice Notes (your phone), Screenshots

My Five Categories Quick Reference

1. Research - Like my friend who googles everything before buying
2. Writing - Like the friend who makes your messy thoughts shine

3. Systems - Like the friend who automates what you do manually
4. Creative - Like the friend who sees possibilities everywhere
5. Strategic - Like the friend who asks the game-changing questions

Note: These categories often blend together in real projects. You might start with Research to understand a topic, move to Creative for brainstorming, then shift to Strategic for planning—all in one conversation. Think of these as starting points, not rigid boxes.

ABOUT THE AUTHOR

Wanjiku Kamau spent twenty years in corporate America at companies including Siemens, Intel, and Google, clinging to her BlackBerry long after everyone else had moved on to smartphones. If you've ever felt behind on technology, she knows the feeling. She lived it.

Getting laid off shocked her, but it also cracked open a door to a chapter she never imagined. That unexpected ending became the catalyst to re-imagine her entire career—and dive into the technology she'd been avoiding.

A first-generation Kenyan American born and raised in the San Francisco Bay Area, Wanjiku holds a Bachelor of Political Science from San Diego State University and an Executive MBA from Arizona State University. She now runs TealBridge, offering consulting and fractional executive services, and TealVoice, where she develops creative projects, including The Dating Mosaic podcast (launching January 2026).

Her journey from frantically Googling AI acronyms to actually understanding this stuff makes her the perfect guide for anyone who feels late to the technology party. She's living proof that you don't need to be a tech genius to figure this out—you just need to be willing to start.

She lives in New York City with her dog Champ, who is terrified of butterflies but fearless on escalators. Out of the Loop, Into the Algorithm is her first book, and she's excited to help others discover that being late doesn't mean you've missed out.

CONNECT WITH WANJIKU

Thank you for reading my story. I'd love to hear yours. Whether you're just starting your AI journey or you're already building something amazing, I'm here to cheer you on. Share your wins, your questions, your spectacular failures—I promise I've been there too.

Find me online:

Book Website: MakingFriendsWithAI.com
Share your AI breakthrough moments, ask questions, and connect with other readers who are figuring this out alongside you.

TealVoice: tealvoice.com
* My creative studio, home of The Dating Mosaic podcast and other storytelling projects.

The Dating Mosaic Podcast: thedatingmosaic.com
Launching January 2026 - Real stories about dating in New York City. Because everyone has a story worth telling. Find The Dating Mosaic on Apple Podcasts, Spotify, and everywhere you listen.

LinkedIn: linkedin.com/in/wanjikukamau
Let's connect professionally. I'd love to hear how you're using AI in your work.

If this book helped you feel a little less intimidated, a little more capable, or gave you permission to start where you are—that's exactly what I hoped for.

Your journey with AI will look different from mine. That's the point.

Now go build something amazing. And when you do, I hope you'll let me know.

With gratitude,

Wanjiku Kamau

DISCLAIMERS

Personal Stories and Privacy

This book is based on the author's personal experiences and recollections. Some names and identifying details have been changed to protect the privacy of individuals. All persons who appear under their real names have provided written permission for their inclusion in this work.

Product References

References to AI tools, platforms, software, and services throughout this book are based solely on the author's personal experience and are provided for educational and informational purposes only. These references do not constitute endorsements, recommendations, or professional advice. The author has no financial relationships, sponsorships, or partnerships with any of the companies or products mentioned unless explicitly stated otherwise.

The AI landscape changes rapidly. Tools, features, pricing, and availability mentioned in this book may have changed since publication. Readers should conduct their own research and due diligence before adopting any tools or services.

Not Professional Advice

This book shares personal experiences and perspectives. It does not constitute professional advice—legal, financial, medical, technical, or otherwise. Readers should consult qualified professionals for advice specific to their situations.

Accuracy and Liability

While the author has made every effort to ensure accuracy, she makes no representations or warranties regarding the completeness or accuracy of the information contained in this book. The author and publisher shall not be liable for any loss, damage, or inconvenience caused as a result of reliance on information contained in this book.

Individual Results

The author's experiences with AI tools are personal and may not be representative of typical results. Individual experiences will vary based on numerous factors including technical expertise, specific use cases, and the evolving nature of AI technology.